Editorial

On 30 June the British Library management made a commitment to its staff and to library users. It would become 'an actively anti-racist organisation', altering its governance and its policies to honour this objective. Roly Keating, the Library's chief executive, spoke of effecting a 'generational shift', to make the institution representative of the nation's diversity in its staffing, its collections and the users it serves. 'There have been incremental changes over the years,' he said, but the murder of George Floyd and its aftermaths was 'a wake-up call for the Library's leadership that it's not enough. Our duty at this moment is to show humility, to listen, to learn and then to enact change.'

Immediately the issue of BAME representation within the executive management and senior curatorial staff was addressed, and 'the urgent and overdue need to reckon fully and openly with the colonial origins and legacy of some of the Library's historic collections and practices.' The Library was in a hurry: '[T]o address these issues, the Library will fund and implement an Anti-Racism action plan, with recommendations developed over the next two months by a Working Group including members of the BAME Staff Network, which has played a leading role in highlighting institutional issues of racial inequality, along with other staff members drawn from across the Library.' The Chief Librarian Liz Jolly lamented how far behind the library had got: '[W]e haven't done enough to ensure that this organisation is anti-racist, and I apologise for that. In convening the Anti-Racism Working Group this is our chance to get it right.'

All this was commendable and timely: the Library set out to recognise and empower people who should have been empowered long ago.

The initiative to name and shame the literary descendants of unsound ancestors, those who had links to the slave trade and colonial exploitation, would 'make a difference' in a very visible way. I came late to the news of the British Library exposé that turned into a damaging ricochet. In November the Library issued a press release and a spreadsheet detailing more than 300 literary figures with 'evidence of connections to slavery, profits from slavery or from colonialism'. It was the product of Printed Heritage Provenance Research, and the brief it had given itself seems to have been unduly capacious. Use every man after his ancestors' deserts, and who should scape whipping?

A British Library spokesman declared: 'In response to growing scholarly interest worldwide, and in common with best practice in other major heritage collections in the UK and worldwide, the British Library's Printed Heritage Collections curatorial team has been conducting a continuing programme of research to ensure that our users have an accurate understanding of those parts of the collections which have direct connections with slavery and other aspects of colonial history. [...] Initial findings from this research, which are subject to further review, have been made available on the British Library's website.'

He went on to highlight one instance in particular. 'In addition to these direct connections, curators have noted some other instances where researchers may wish to be aware that an "associate" or indirect connection can be made, through family history or otherwise. One such instance is the reference to Nicholas Ferrar (1592–1637), a distant ancestor of English poet and writer Ted Hughes, which is included solely for the sake of completeness and accuracy, and is not, of course, intended in any way whatsoever to affect the reputation of Hughes himself. [...] Ted Hughes was a major figure in twentieth-century English poetry and the British Library is proud to be custodian of one of the world's finest archival resources for the study of his work.' Ted Hughes was just one of the 300 individuals fingered.

George Orwell was another. I am told that Byron and Wilde were also on the spreadsheet.

I looked for the spreadsheet online to get a sense of its wider scope, its terms and methods, and to see which scholars were assembling the dossier of the directly implicated, those with an 'associate' or 'indirect connection', and those included 'otherwise'. It was not to be found on the Library website. It had also disappeared from social media where it had been widely discussed and seemed to have become invisible.

What had happened? A public and widely publicised 'exposure' intended to demonstrate the staunch spirit of the new British Library had managed to 'cancel' itself. Moral enforcers are hard on individuals who seek to retract and excuse ill-considered statements or actions: it leaves a permanent blemish on their reputation. But if the ill-considered statement or action proceeds from the enforcers themselves, the situation is differently handled. The British Library, our main copyright library, the most authoritative public record in the land, with its welcome undertakings on diversity, transparency and answerability, erased its 'error' and the record of it.

I still have not been able to get to the bottom of it, but the bottom of it is where we need to get. I wrote to the Library: 'Can you point me to the full list and explanatory text of Printed Heritage Provenance Research in which Ted Hughes was erroneously included? I would like to see it and can't trace it within the BL website.' Then I wrote again. 'I am concerned about the spread of cancel culture and the damage to a lot of people in our "sector" of false or maliciously construed or misconstrued connections. Is it possible to get access to the list of 300 allegedly implicated parties and any of the documentation surrounding the project? Whose initiative was it; if not an individual's, then which committee? It's unfortunate how allegations stick, even when their inaccuracy is revealed and apologies are issued.'

The reply I received was simple. 'We've taken the list down now, so I can't send it to you now I'm afraid,' a Library employee replied.

On 25 November the *Guardian* carried a report: the Library had retracted the list and apologised to Ted Hughes's widow. That left 299 other figures 'whose collections were associated with wealth obtained from colonial violence' and whose executors or descendants could not speak for them. No doubt there was some substance in the list and in some of the underlying scholarship that we must assume went into it, but the damage of the list, and then of its retraction, will take some time and effort to repair. Some process for reviewing research must be implemented without delay. The Library admitted that 'early presentation of these findings has caused confusion and concern, particularly in relation to connections drawn between named individuals and their ancestors'. It still has the institutional knack of understatement and obfuscation in its public statements. Having slapped its own wrist for failure in implementing diversity policies, it is doing its best to hush up another failure, of supervision and research. Hughes scholar Jonathan Bate commented, 'Over-zealousness of this kind undoes the important work of excavating the history of the institutions that have benefited from slavery – it plays into the hands of both the "cancel culture" and the "anti-woke" press.' As was indeed the case.

How does its subsequent action, behind its grand closed doors, tally with Roly Keating's commitment – 'Our duty at this moment is to show humility, to listen, to learn and then to enact change'?

News and Notes

Language and Power

Sasha Dugdale writes: Don Mee Choi's *DMZ Colony* (Wave Books, 2020) has won the 2020 National Book Award for Poetry. *DMZ Colony* is a book-length work, and the second book in a trilogy, which began with Choi's *Hardly War* in 2016.

Don Mee's body of work is concerned with language, history and geopolitics. The title, *DMZ Colony*, refers to the demilitarised zone between North and South Korea, and one of the central episodes in the work is an interview the author conducted with a Korean 'Communist sympathiser' Ahn Hak-sop who lives in the DMZ and who was treated brutally by the authorities in South Korea. Other episodes recreate the voices of orphans who witnessed genocide by the South Korean army and women who have been beaten until their skin was blue (this last account is accompanied by sketches of thousands of tiny blue angels). The episodes are interspersed by text, images, personal reminiscences and profound and yet delicate meditations on language and power.

In work remarkable for its fluidity, beauty and operatic qualities, Don Mee Choi traces the political nature of language, and reveals how language itself is formed and deformed by relationships of political power and landscapes of war and colonialisation. As one of the pre-eminent Korean-English translators, Don Mee has written movingly about the act of translation between two modes of being, especially when translation is performed across the fissures of neo-colonialism (as Don Mee describes the relationship between the USA and South Korea). Here that awareness is embodied in disjointed and dreamlike dialogue and the coming together of both languages in one fractured twin-self.

Much has been written about the politics of Don Mee Choi's groundbreaking work: the two books are unique in their seamless blending of the personal, the political and the historical. But nothing in Don Mee's work is naked polemic. She begins very simply from her own fractured, exiled language-self and builds outwards, constructing structures of thought, word and expression, just as she painstakingly constructed the many mulberry-paper angels that formed part of a recent exhibition of her visual work in Berlin. The result is a book for our age, a radical (in that it builds from the roots out) philosophy, a new angel of history backing away slowly from the wreck of the century.

When thou hast Donne

The British Library has acquired – 'saved for the nation' as they say – a seventeenth-century manuscript of John Donne's poetry. The 'Melford Hall manuscript' is accessible online for everyone and will be available to researchers through the British Library's Reading Rooms in 2021.

The manuscript was discovered in Melford Hall, Suffolk in 2018. It includes over 130 poems by Donne and is one of the five largest collections of scribal copies of Donne material surviving. It includes famous verse such as 'The Calme', 'To his Mistress Going to Bed', 'The Breake of Daye' and 'Sunn Risinge'. Created in the early seventeenth century, the 400-page volume features text written in iron gall ink on gilt edged paper and is bound in a quarto gilt panelled calf binding with an oval centrepiece. Donne's poems were often copied out in manuscript for circulation among aficionados rather than being published for a general readership.

The British Library's acquisition was supported by a grant from the National Heritage Memorial Fund (NHMF) and funding from the British Library Collections Trust, the Friends of the National Libraries and the American Trust for the British Library.

Dr Alexander Lock, Curator of Modern Archives and Manuscripts at the British Library, said: 'The British Library's mission is to make our intellectual heritage accessible to everyone and the discovery of this collection of poems presents a major new resource for scholarship. The Melford Hall manuscript provides evidence as to how Donne's poetry was written, copied and circulated, as well as helping to further shape our understanding of his audiences and patrons.'

A Covid open letter from Shakespeare & Co., Paris

Dear Friends, Thank you so much to the many of you who reached out after our last newsletter asking how you can help the bookshop. It is true that, like many independent businesses, we are struggling, trying to see a way forward during this time when we've been operating at a loss, with our sales down almost 80% since March.

With this in mind, we would be especially grateful for new website orders from those of you with the means and interest to do so. Below, we've compiled some of our favorite books and merchandise, including our new Le Sac Shopping, made from 100% recycled plastic. And we're thrilled to announce the opening of enrollment to our 2021 Year of

Reading, an annual subscription whereby we mail parcels of books and gifts to you from Paris throughout the year.

Next year will mark seven decades since our bookshop first opened its doors. Today, each morning, taking down the wooden shutters, opening those same doors, and welcoming readers and writers – whether travellers from across the world or the Parisians who are still able to visit us – always feels like an immense privilege. Because, as well as being a bookshop, Shakespeare and Company is a community, a commune (often literally), of which you are all a part. We are here today, almost seventy years after that first morning, because of you.

We send our best wishes for your health and safety. May we all thrive together soon. With thanks & love, Shakespeare and Company

Happily, the letter of invitation had the desired effect and the bookshop received a mighty surge of support and seems to have weathered the storm and emerged as vigorous and irreplaceable as ever.

Poetry Archive Now! Wordview 2020

Maggie Sullivan, administrator of the Poetry Archive, writes: The Poetry Archive opened its doors wide and invited poets from around the world to submit work in the form of a homemade video on topics informing their writing during 2020. Before we knew it, the world was forced to close many of its doors and our project took on a whole new dimension. More than 370 poets from 22 countries around the world sent in work for our YouTube channel. Our judges, Imtiaz Dharker, Robert Seatter and Lavinia Singer, chose twenty entries for a Winners' Collection on the Poetry Archive website. You can access our YouTube channel and Winners' collection using this link: https://poetryarchive.org/collections/wordview-2020/.

Emyr Humphreys (1919–2020)

Sam Adams writes: Emyr Humphreys, the distinguished novelist, poet and cultural historian, died on 29 September 2020 at his home in Llanfairpwll, Anglesey. He was 101. *Shards of Light*, his last book and third collection of poems (reviewed in *PNR* 249, 2019), was a remarkable centenary triumph. He was a man of gentle demeanour and strong principle – Christian, humanitarian, rootedly Welsh. A conscientious objector in WWII, he helped succour the human wreckage of military campaigns in North Africa and Italy as a charity worker for the Save the Children Fund, acquiring his third language, Italian, and a staunch European outlook in the process. He was born in the anglicised north-east corner of Wales and the Welsh that was to become the language of his home and social life he learned as a teenager while studying history at UCW Aberystwyth, at the same time as he acquired his commitment to Wales as a nation. Aside from his writing, his career embraced periods as a teacher, in broadcasting and as an academic. He wrote plays in Welsh for S4C, the Welsh-language TV channel for which he had campaigned vigorously, but English remained the medium of the greater part of his creative output. He published twenty-four novels, including the seven-volume sequence 'Land of the Living' and his master-piece, *Outside the House of Baal*.

Nathan Zach (1930–2020)

Anthony Rudolf writes: Nathan Zach, who died recently within a month of his ninetieth birthday, was by this time the senior Israeli poet. Born in Berlin in 1930, he was six years younger than the late Yehuda Amichai, also born in Germany. Unlike Amichai, Zach was not from a religious family, and unlike Amichai he did not become internationally celebrated among the wider poetry-reading public. Amichai, like Ginsberg and Neruda, was a prodigious maker of poems, a ceaseless producer of song and chant, equally sophisticated but more popular in tone than Zach. Which is not to say that Zach

was an elite poet difficult of access. On the contrary, he, like the USA born T. Carmi and the Bukovina-born Dan Pagis and the *sabra* Moshe Dor, wrote deceptively conversational lyrics. No one spoke like that in real life but during the time of the poem, as in a play or a novel, readers are persuaded by the artifice that they are overhearing a lucid and brilliant talker: the illusion is achieved by mastery of free verse rhythm, subtle syntax, repetition, tonal sophistication, crucial enjambements: pitch-perfect musicality of simulacra, great as-ifs: he deployed most registers of modern poetry and created a great *oeuvre*. It works as subject matter because of the artifice, complexity made apparently simple. Take away the sophisticated poetical work with language, and you would have jottings.

Zach was of a generation that came after the Russian and East European-influenced Hebrew poets such as Shlonsky and Alterman, *kibbutz* poets who arrived in the 1920s and whose modernism was deemed antiquated by the poets who came to maturity in the 1950s. Zach, unlike Amichai, edited avant-garde magazines and wrote influential iconoclastic articles, killing the senior gods. His influences were German (as we might expect) and Anglo-American, including Auden and Eliot, Ginsberg and Lowell. His first translator into English was Jon Silkin, who published him in a Northern House pamphlet. Between these two (born in the same year) there was reciprocal influence, and Silkin, the finest Anglo-Jewish poet since Rosenberg, is probably his closest English equivalent.

Zach lived in London for most of the 1970s while studying and teaching at the University of Essex where his friends included the poet and scholar John Barrell. His friends in London included myself, when we both lived in Belsize Park. There was talk of a Menard Press book, which came to nothing, but I obviously included him in *Voices in the Ark*, my world anthology of Jewish poets co-edited with Howard Schwartz and published in the USA in 1980; although, unlike Amichai, Zach did not rejoice in the possibilities available to a lover of, if not necessarily practitioner of, Jewish tradition. Nor did he go to the other extreme, that of the so-called Canaanite poets and he was not self-consciously avant-garde like David Avidan. Later there were books and selections in translation by Peter Everwhine, Peter Cole and others.

On one visit to Israel, I bumped into Zach in Haifa (where he was for years a professor at the university) outside the Bahai temple, close to his house, and sadly he was a little the worse for wear. Poetry and the demon alcohol. Zach arrived in Mandate Palestine, aged six, in 1936. By the time of his death he had won all the major literary Israeli prizes and many international honours. He participated in the 1948 War of Independence. As a pro-Palestinian activist and politico, his politics were way to the left of the liberal socialists well known outside Israel such as Oz and Grossman. In mainstream circles, the politics aroused as much hostility as his poetics had earlier. Even so, he was eulogised by the President of Israel. His final years were blighted by Alzheimers; the domestic circumstances were much discussed in the press as was his long and complicated relationship with Amichai, whose first book he published when they were close colleagues and friends.

His many books include a translation of Ginsberg's *Kaddish* and various German plays. Before his long decline, at his best, he was, like Yehuda Amichai, a charming and brilliant man. But Nathan was more reserved, more intellectual. However, what matters to those who did not have the privilege of knowing him is that he was one of the most important Hebrew poets of the last third of the twentieth century and deserves as much attention as the slightly older and more prolific Amichai. These two major poets, born in Germany, shadowed each other in life, in work and now in death. Rich is the literature which contains two such contemporaries.

Diane di Prima (1934–2020)

Diane di Prima, the noted Feminist and quondam Beat poet, was born in Brooklyn, attended Swarthmore College but moved to Greenwich Village where she completed her education and emergence. She became a friend of Baraka, Ginsberg, Kerouac, O'Hara and Audre Lorde. For a time she belonged to Timothy Leary's 'intentional community' in upstate New York, then moved to San Francisco in 1968.

In her work, politics and spiritual practice sometimes fuse, and her formal interests sometimes work in a suggestive dissonance with her preferred stream of consciousness voice. She was a kind of Buddhist, and she helped set up the San Francisco Institute of Magical and Healing Arts. A writer, mother and activist, she once told an interviewer, 'I wanted everything – very earnestly and totally – I wanted to have every experience I could have, I wanted everything that was possible to a person in a female body, and that meant that I wanted to be mother.... [...] "Well, nobody's done it quite this way before but fuck it, that's what I'm doing, I'm going to risk it."'

She published forty books, some with manifesto-like metaphorical titles: *This Kind of Bird Flies Backward* (1958) and *Loba* (1978, 1998). Her early *Memoirs of a Beatnik* (1968) was oblique but candid, and *Recollections of My Life as a Woman: The New York Years* (2001) relived the same, intense formative years in which, with Baraka, she edited *The Floating Bear (1961–69)*.

She received the National Poetry Association's Lifetime Service Award and enjoyed grants from the National Endowment for the Arts and other money-dispensing bodies. She taught at the Jack Kerouac School of Disembodied Poetics at the Naropa Institute and elsewhere.

Lewis Warsh (1944–2020)

David Rosenberg writes: Born 1944 in New York, Lewis Warsh died there, 15 November 2020. He was a pillar of 2nd Generation New York School, as poet, novelist and editor of *Angel Hair, The World* and Angel Hair Books with his first wife, poet Anne Waldman, and *United Artists*, mag and books, with his second wife, poet Bernadette Mayer. Attended in hospice by his beloved wife of twenty years, Katt, she called when Lewis lost control of his hands in his last days, putting him on the line, his voice as strong as ever, and worried, the most worried, inquiring voice I've known beside my mother's. Not about us *per se* but about our ability to nail down a moment in history. Of course, nothing was 'nailed down' except Lewis's voice in my ear and in the communal ear, for which it is a loving deadpan. '"LOVE POEMS" / by Frank O'Hara / (it's never far off) / Take me down, it says from the shelf / take me down / take me down down / & open / & open me / & open me.' (1972). It is closest perhaps to Ted Berrigan, the presiding influence of our generation in his provocative range of humorous open-heart surgery. From 'Train Ride' (1971, reprinted 2020 by Vehicle Editions): 'I rent a car & drive it to Wales, & Liverpool, / with / Lewis Warsh, / on Acid!'

His family emigrated from Vilna, Lithuania ('the Jerusalem of the East'). Lewis showed little evidence in his writing of his Jewish background or family drama. This was in opposition to his lifelong interrogation of history itself, manifesting in his mid-twenties in *Part of My History,* which I edited at Coach House Press. Rereading it now, I'm struck by its attention, in alternating prose and poetry, strictly to physical movement: who was coming and going within his immediate vicinity. It was more strangely domesticated than Frank O'Hara's informal (though brilliantly timed) sashaying in verse, our New York School master.

By then, Lewis's work was known in Canada as a regular contributor to *The Ant's Forefoot*, distributed also in England by Andrew Crozier's Ferry Press. Tom Raworth, Lee Harwood, John James, and Wendy Mulford asked after him.

Lewis's first posthumous book, a new edition of his translation of Robert Desnos's *Night of Loveless Nights*, will appear from Ugly Duckling Presse.

Reports

Stillness with Trees, and Plurilocalism
Vahni Capildeo

Stillness is not a quality I associate with trees, or with the human body. Trees are naturally dynamic. They conduct lightning; they drop branches. Saman trees, or rain trees, are conspicuous for their huge canopies of fine, darkish leaves which muddle dusken skylines, easily being mistaken for a portion of hill or thundercloud. A saman tree used to grow next to the driveway of my parents' house. It began to compete for upper airspace with the television aerial. Whenever hurricanes were in the area, we assessed the pitch of its tossing. Its root system ploughed up the driveway. We could see asphalt furrows radiating closer and closer towards the house and knew that roots were underneath.

Once, when I was out in the yard, the sky turned pale and the birds made a special, remote screeching as they flocked upward to the higher branches of the saman tree. The ground underfoot began to shake like thick split pea soup in an iron pot. I felt my legs being moved. I looked up and saw the tree being moved, just like me, but in a much bigger fashion. At that moment I was not checking for falling branches but looking for companionship. I was afraid of the tree, and sorry when it eventually was cut down. As for my body, it treats me to a continuous sound and light show: everything from migraine auras to tinnitus. An heroic effort to empty the mind is all very well, but what if one's own body takes the side of distraction?

The fallacy, of course, is that quiet consists in self-forgetfulness, or in dissociation from one's environment. Silence is one of the themes of my research for the next two years, and I am convinced that surround sound is one of the possible conditions that enable surround silence; in fact, surround silence and surround sound may be functionally the same. When deep in the right kind of noise, it is possible to enjoy drifting into a type of stillness, like the comparative weightlessness of a swimmer who allows themself to float.

I remember agreeing to go with a friend on a silent meditation walk in the grounds of an old house in Oxfordshire which had been converted into a retreat centre. I was curious about the house, and this was one way of getting to see it. Silence, and meditation, were too normal a part of my life for either of those to be the draw. The silent meditation walk was guided. It was a startling experience. The group could not speak, but the guide could. A mishmash of chatter fills my head as I try to bring the scene into focus in my memory: 'Now look at this tree. Really look at the tree. Be with the tree. Be present to the tree. Look at the leaves. Are you looking at the leaves? Find a leaf. Look at the leaf. Do you ever stop to look at leaves? When was the last time you stopped to look at a leaf? Now keep on looking at that leaf...' He was comfortable in the absence of answers. I was astounded that anyone could say versions of the same thing so many times. This is an unfair and selectively edited memory, but sometimes it comes up when I am standing silently with a tree, and I laugh... He was intent on calling our attention to being attentive, so it was impossible to tune him out and make him part of the surround sound; I tuned into neither inner silence nor surround silence.

Silence and quiet are not the same. In the last seven months of writing *Like a Tree, Walking*, my new book of poems for Carcanet Press, I practised stillness and listening exercises, first alone in a room, then with students, finally outdoors in the company of trees. These exercises do not hyper-sensitise or switch off awareness. They enable the practitioner to note and name the types and levels of sound, from outermost to innermost, and thus become aware of oneself as a still thing, placed in sound. I decided to make the exercises site-specific and in a way dialogic; certain trees or clumps of trees would provide the environment, including how they altered the soundscape either by sounds of their making, or how sounds bounced off them, or how people sounded differently in manoeuvring around them.

We are not less 'present' if the soundscape in which we physically are mixes with the soundscapes which we remember having inhabited. While I often write about the ordinariness of plurilingualism (even among so-called monoglots), lately I have been fascinated with the idea that everyday experience is plurilocal as well as plurilingual. When invited by the Auralities research group at the University of Cambridge to speak on the 'poetics of place and displacement', I wanted to sketch out aspects of my new working approach to memory of place and memory in place, with particular reference to sound, silence and imagination. This took the form of three main observations.

First, who carries displacement, and how? It is impossible to judge from looking at people. Consider intersectionality and violent displacement, in terms of the individual. Someone who seems to have emigrated for love, or economic reasons, or education – someone who seems well-set-up and easily pigeonholed – may well have moved for other motives. They may have fled domestic abuse or discrimination on sexual or religious grounds, and not wanted or been able to document this. They may have a trauma history. In that case, *they are still fleeing*, because their reasons for flight, in remaining unspoken, continually find other ways of being told. How such 'double emigrants' weave their way into their new place, and how they narrate their old place, are manifestations of *silence*, both selective, chosen silence and painful silencing.

This brings me to another way that displacement is carried in the soundscape, and to my second observation. Violent displacement has been widespread for centuries under colonialism (in other contexts as well, but I speak from this one). Transgenerational displacement remains lived and remains live. People who seem to be smoothed into an 'identity' nevertheless may be marked affectively by such histories... in readiness to take flight, quickness to shut down, expectations of being moved

on, suspected, or killed. As for the soundscape: everyday mispronunciations or hyperassimilated versions of one's name, for example, can add to the normalisation of mild alienation as a way of being. One becomes other in repeatedly being named, called, otherwise. You are named *into* conversation at an angle from where you would name yourself. The sound of how you are called places you strangely.

The third observation is that there are consequences for sound in place... and for the differential translation of the soundscape of a place. The accent or language of one's diaspora may be 'triggering', if heard, say, in the street. Imagine being expected to identify with or even delight in the vocal music of the perpetrators from whom you fled... Less negatively, though also ruinously, imagine experiencing sudden acute pockets of loss, a sense of bereavement that is too exilic to attain nostalgia. You might hear, passing in the street, fragments of a beloved ancestral language which had been spoken fluently by grandparents, recited formally by parents, but which is inaccessible, meaningless except as loss, because schooled out of oneself or never learnt because denied by the wider context of one's never *post*-colonial education. It would be socially disruptive to keep mentioning this to friends *not* feeling language loss. Once more, whatever is heard or spoken by the inheritor of displacement participates in doubleness and silence.

Consider, too, the perception of volume and intensity. Words or music may register with undue or inexpressible force for associative reasons such as those named above, associations with personal or historical displacements. Then the inner ear does not hear 'the same' soundscape as others. The volume goes up and down, the sound environment fades out or overwhelms. Listening transforms into a process of adjustment, apart from hearing. Is such a hearer and listener more sensitised and more fatigued? What is the residual or somatic effect of being displaced as a hearer while apparently being in place as a listener and interlocutor? What about the eye? What about seeing scripts from ancestral languages or 'friend' or 'enemy' languages, and perhaps knowing how to sound them but not what they mean, or not knowing how to sound them but understanding them in terms of a cultural meaning? The environment becomes noisy, thin, and saturated by this multiple translation and translatability of the visible into the audible.

To explore what I term 'plurilocalism', the state in which whatever place one happens to be in is referred to and through other *specific* places, whether known personally or known only as lost, I began in the safe environment of trees. They helped me sense how the ecology of transplant hearing might find formal and disruptive shape on the page.

Wavering

Anne Stevenson, 1933–2020

JOHN LUCAS

I've always thought that there were three factors essential to Anne Stevenson's poetry. One, her father was a philosopher, two, that during her early years she harboured a desire to be a musician, and three, that although she was born in Cambridge, England, in 1933, where Charles Stevenson was for a year pursuing his research, she spent her early years in Harvard, and then Yale. Then, in 1945, her father was dismissed from Yale because of what Anne's widower husband, Peter Lucas (no relation), reports was his 'unamerican rejection of absolute values', which led to the charge that he was corrupting the morals of the young. From an early age, Anne must have been accustomed to an atmosphere in which the life of the intellect was taken for granted, as well as a wariness about language and its absolutist claims. The fact that Charles and Louise Stevenson played host to the great philosopher, Ernst Cassirer, who, like so many Jewish intellectuals, had escaped from Hitler's Germany, must have helped nourish this atmosphere.

A house of talk, of skeptical enquiry, a house of two pianos, a house filled with music. When Matt Simpson and I put together a festschrift for Anne's seventieth birthday we were lent a photograph of her as a young teenager, bent over the cello, intent, concentrated. And I imagine that throughout her adult life she was never far from a piano. There was one in the cottage in North Wales where she and Peter spent months at a time, in later years, and one in her study at their home in Durham where, even after she had been gripped by a profound deafness – it was for a while alleviated by a cochlear implant – she continued to practise. And during the memorial occasion for the poet and exhibition designer Arnold Rattenbury, I remember noticing that Anne was fingering on her thigh the notes of a Mozart sonata as it was played on stage by Bernard Roberts.

In an essay-memoir, she says that her father's 'superb' reading of poems to her when she was a girl profoundly affected her. 'It was the rhythm, the stressed, unstressed undulations, of the iambic line, that first bewitched me.' And she adds that 'almost always, some overheard musical cadence starts me writing'. Anyone who heard her read her own poems will know how finely she gave utterance to them. In an essay I wrote for a collection of critical essays on her, *Voyages over Voices*, edited by Angela Leighton, I remarked how Anne's delight in polysyllabic words freed her to use hovering stresses as part of a poem's intrinsic, variable rhythms, and I added that these made possible a *rubato* effect, one that serves perfectly the serious playfulness of such a phrase as 'infinitesimal capillaries'. (See her poem 'The Spirit is too Blunt an Instrument'.) Anne Stevenson may be a formalist, but she isn't at all constrained by her use of stanza, rhyme and line length. She uses them; they don't use her. And in this she is, of course, in that New England tradition – of hymn, psalm, the King James Bible – that runs from Dickinson through Frost to Elizabeth Bishop.

Bishop, above all. In the Preface to her book-length *Five Looks at Elizabeth Bishop* (1998), she writes that 'More than any other contemporary, Elizabeth Bishop opened my eyes to possibilities and directions for poetry I might never have explored without her example.' She also acknowledges that the separate essays that constitute the book are between them an attempt to make up for what she thinks of as the inadequacy of an earlier 'Introduction' to Bishop's work, published in 1965. My wife and I were staying with Anne and Peter at their cottage at the time of the book's publication, and when she gave us an inscribed copy Anne included with it a typed copy of a then brand new poem, 'Arioso Dolente', which would appear in her next collection, *Granny Scarecrow* (2003). Underneath the title is a dedication: 'For my grandchildren when they become grandparents' – and the poem itself begins with recollections of her parents before moving on to a memory of her grandmother. These memories are themselves woken, so the poem insists, by the young poet's remembrance of how, as she sat practising Beethoven's sonata, her father, running downstairs, instructed her:

> G!
>
> D natural, C flat! *Dolente, arioso –*
> Put all the griefs of the world in that change of key.

There were griefs in Beethoven's life, there will be griefs in the poet's, there are griefs, real or potential, in all lives. But 'Consciousness walks on tiptoe through what happens. / So much is felt, so little of it said.'

In his splendid account of this major poem, John Greening remarks that 'Anne Stevenson's great strength as a poet is her refusal to lose her concentration, her determination to sustain a thought, an intuition to its very end.' (*The Way You Say the World*, p.41.) Art bears testimony to sustained concentration, and there is no doubt that for Stevenson it is Elizabeth Bishop whose art best exemplifies such concentration. 'Arioso Dolente' doesn't dwindle into nostalgia, as Greening says, any more than do other Stevenson poems, long or short.

By the time she came to write that poem, Stevenson had shrugged off an element of portentousness that occasionally marred the earlier work. This is especially true of *Correspondences* (1974), which, compelling though it is, is painfully self-conscious about the demands made on poets, a matter far more adroitly handled in 'Making Poetry', a poem she published a decade later in *The Fiction Makers* (1985). Here, she speaks of the need to 'evade the ego-hill, the misery well, / the siren hiss of *publish / success, publish / success, success, success*'.

There is an element of self-rebuke in this, but it is also directed at other poets; contemporaries, in particular, who not only draw their art from the misery well but expect to be applauded for doing so. (She has a sharp little piece about Anne Sexton, who, having given a reading of her work at its most confessional/harrowing, stood on stage to receive a bouquet of flowers and, like any diva, bowed and waved to her audience.)

This inevitably brings us to the vexed matter of Sylvia Plath. In his essay on 'Stevenson's Elegies for Plath', Adam Piette quotes a remark from the planned epilogue to *Bitter Fame,* where the author asks 'Which of Plath's contemporaries, including myself, can honestly admit to having *not* been envious of those last poems?' This is entirely honest, and I agree with Piette when he adds that, for Stevenson, 'the fifty-five- year-old survivor and mature woman, the envy is tempered by critique.' (*Voyages Over Voices,* p.65.) But the furore that followed the biography's appearance in 1989 made plain that for most critics *any* adverse comment Anne made about Plath must have been motivated by green-eyed jealousy. She was shaken by the rancour. She told me that the American poet, W.S. ('Bill') Merwin, had warned her off from agreeing to write the book. 'Bad karma,' Merwin said, 'bad karma.'

Plath was not Sexton, of course, nor did Anne suggest that she was. But her opponents didn't see it that way. It says a great deal for her resolve, her refusal to sink into the misery well, that although she once ruefully spoke of the three wasted years she spent on *Bitter Fame*, the following decade saw the publication of two major collections, *Four and a Half Dancing Men* (1993) and *Granny Scarecrow* (2000). And in between, in 1996, Oxford University Press published *The Collected Poems of Anne Stevenson 1955–1995.* In fact, the 1990s was an unusually productive decade, given that, as well as the poetry, Anne published *Between the Iceberg and the Ship: Selected Essays* (Ann Arbor, Michigan, 1998), and, in the same year, *Five Looks at Elizabeth Bishop* (Agenda/Bellow, Poets on Poetry, London.)

As for Bishop, so for Stevenson, looking is of primary importance. What most concerns her, she says, is Bishop's 'insistence on *looking* at the world and finding there solid correlatives for the marvels, griefs and contradictions that shaped her personal geography'. And this is consonant with Stevenson's own concerns. Like Bishop, she was displaced by geography from home and familiar circumstance, and this gave a special quality to her ways of looking. Seeing as an outsider allowed her to observe, for instance, the strangeness of English ways, which she writes about with acerbic, observational wit when, soon after her arrival in England in the early 1950s, she married into a family keen to uphold its social position, as a result of which one would-be bridesmaid chosen by Anne had to be shoehorned out from her role. The family Anne was marrying into made evident that the young woman's Northern accent simply 'wouldn't do'.

Throughout her career, poems about the strangeness of her adopted country recur. A number of these are gathered together in a section called 'England' in *Poems 1955–2005*, though the decision not to give the dates for any of poems that make up this Bloodaxe Collected

means we can't follow the gathering intensity of what is essentially a Darwinistic regard for the phenomenal.

Over the years this regard becomes essential to her work. Hence, for example, 'Pity the Birds', which details:

> rapacious Mrs Blackbird shopping on foot
>   in the hedges,
> even yesterday's warbler, lying stiff on the step
>   to the barn,
> olive green wings torn awry by the wind
>   eyes gone,
> but with tri-clawed reptilian feet still
>   hungrily curled.

> Not one of them gened to protest
>   against the world.

Living for months at a time in mountainous North Wales strengthened, she said, her sense of the longevity of the universe, the brief temporality of animate existence. She was not discomforted by this, nor the acknowledgement of nature's indifference to the human. When I sent her an essay I'd written for the journal, *Raceme,* about Frost's 'The Most of It' and Bishop's 'The Moose', she disagreed with my reading of the 'great buck's' significance in Frost's poem. The man in the poem, Anne said, who's 'virtually Everyman', in calling for a unique place in the universe, 'missed the wonder of what he *could* have, the magnificence of the buck'. And so, she goes on, 'Frost and Bishop are on the same side; both distrust any idea of a Creator who made the world with any such idea in mind. Darwin wrote of man's "arrogance" in assuming any such thing.' I don't think we were far apart in our readings of the poem, but Anne's is certainly focused by her Darwinism.

In the last letter I have from her, written in May this year, she comments on the Covid virus, but only to say that by comparison with the England of Hilary Mantel's *The Mirror and the Light,* living in a country of 'panicked lockdown' seems a luxury. And despite saying that she's too tired to write more – her Parkinson's disease was by then advancing remorselessly – she encloses a page of commentary on Larkin's 'Aubade', a poem she finds 'moving and NOT discouraging. Rather the opposite, in fact'. The poem, she says, is Larkin's last masterpiece, and 'although its subject, the poet's fear of death, is unremittingly black, the form is anything but. Any reader with an ear is captivated by the form: five elegant stanzas of ten iambic pentameter lines, each one rhyming... The absolutely clear, conversational diction is handled with a metaphorical dexterity that allows for unforgettable lines: "Religion used to try / That vast moth-eaten brocade"; "Meanwhile telephones crouch, getting ready to ring / In locked-up offices" – lines which hardly evoke anything from me but a smile of admiration.' Larkin's poetry, she adds, 'allows for plenty of imagination but not for an escape into fantasy at the expense of reality'.

And then, at the bottom of the page, she adds, 'When I began to write poetry in the shadow of Sylvia Plath, I was under the impression that madness in a poet was a sure sign of a superior talent. Now, in my 80s, I think that although extreme sensitivity or vulnerability may well be forms of madness, I am all for keeping one's balance on the high wire and enjoying as much of the view as is possible in one short span of life.'

Reading these words, written a few, short months before the death of my dear friend, and, far more important, wonderfully good poet, the sadness I feel at her going is offset by what has to be a smile of purest admiration.

'The sea over the land'
W. G. Sebald Faces the North Sea
Iain Bamforth

W.G. Sebald's prose has a spectral, submerged, lulling effect because its true territory is aqueous. And this aqueous element extends not over the low-lying, muddy, featureless estuary of the Thames – 'the old river in its broad reach' – as it winds out of London past generations of wharves and cranes to Gravesend and the Essex marshes and debouches along the low shores of Suffolk to the north, the vista immortalised by Marlow at the opening of Conrad's *Heart of Darkness*, when an entire imperial civilisation and all its dreams of conquest seem to slip into the ooze of time, but over a former stretch of terra firma off the coast of Anglia and now entirely mantled by the sea.

This is the westernmost part of the landmass that once joined the south-eastern coast of the British Isles to the Hook of Holland, north-western Germany and Denmark during and after the last Ice Age. Eighteen thousand years ago, the sea level was considerably lower and tundra extended from the present-day Pas de Calais to the coast of Scotland. The English Channel was the bed of a large river draining south-west into the Atlantic. There was even a freshwater lake in its centre, now known as the Outer Silver Pit, which may have marked the confluence of the some of the great rivers of Europe: the future Maas, Scheldt and Thames. Cenozoic silt deposits in East Anglia suggest that an arm of the Rhine extended as far north as the fens. The contemporary archaeologist Bryony Coles has become well known for her speculative maps of the region based on sonar and seismic survey data, but, already, in 1913, the palaeobiologist Clement Reid was studying Neolithic flints and mammoth bones retrieved from this area, and the Castle Museum in Norwich contains many animal remains and earthly goods retrieved over the years from the submerged peat. Fishermen are still bringing up evidence of the former life of Doggerland in their dragnets; in so doing, it might be observed, acting just like writers.

Sebald writes in his posthumous collection of essays *Campo Santo* that he was fascinated by geography as a child, devoting hours to poring over atlases and brochures. It was a bookish pursuit that persisted into adulthood; he is a topographically precise writer. Although he published an appreciative portrait of the footloose Bruce Chatwin and his ability to turn fragments 'into significant mementos endowed with a wealth of meaning, reminding us of what we, as living beings, cannot reach', he was never an especially exuberant traveller himself, and beyond his attachment to his native Allgäu and the select group of largely Alemannic writers assembled in his posthumous collection *A House in the Country* the trails of many of his journeys seem to narrow down obsessively on this fluent triangle between Britain and north-western Europe. As often as not, he is to be found on the beach south of Lowestoft 'watching the sand martins darting to-and-fro over the sea' or, alternatively, 'looking across to England from a beach in Holland'. It is difficult not to think of Caspar David Friedrich's radically uncompromising painting 'Monk by the Sea' (1809), in which a solitary monk standing on the dunes supports his bare head in his hands while contemplating a sullen sea and leaden sky, welded in menace. Somewhere off the coast lies the buried shelf of his imaginings, a reach where herring and mackerel flash out of the depths – depths now bespoiled with unexploded armaments and the chemical runoffs of agriculture and industry – and leave the surface record of their 'wonderful shimmering appearance'.

So what happened to Doggerland, this extensive lowland of mudflats, embayments, marshes and lagoons that was perhaps the richest hunting ground in Mesolithic times for fish and fowl? As sea levels rose around 8,000 years ago, Doggerland became submerged beneath the epeiric or subcontinental sea the Roman author Pliny would call Septentrionalis Oceanus, and later generations the German Ocean or Noordzee. Rising sea levels may also have been abetted by a catastrophic tsunami known as the Storegga Slide; the melting glaciers of Scotland and Scandinavia, following the period known as the Last Glacial Maximum, are conjectured to have given rise to an enormous impounded freshwater lake whose subsequent outburst surge scoured out the present-day landscape around the Strait of Dover. At any rate, subsequent sea erosion ensured that Britain became physically separated from the continent: separation is thought to have been complete by 6500 BCE, although Doggerland itself may have survived as an island for another millennium. Now, it is a land without landfall.

The North Sea is therefore a comparatively recent aquatic territory. In time, as it sank beneath the waves, Doggerland became the Dogger Bank, a treacherous maritime region of sandbanks in places only twenty metres deep. As an ecological niche it was a prime fishing ground. The early trade of Viking times expanded with King Cnut's short-lived empire and the Hanseatic League in the early Middle Ages to embrace all the lands around the sea: trade routes extended from the Low Countries and Denmark all the way up to Shetland and Arctic Norway. In his book *The Edge of the World*, the historian Michael Pye even makes the case that this cold grey sea 'made the modern world possible'. A remarkable assertion – if we assume that meteorological conditions were more or less as they are now, with barrowloads of clouds in the west, frequent wet squalls and the sun suspended in a strange viscous pall.

Tantalising references to this approximate area occur in several ancient geographers. Pytheas, the early explorer from the Greek city of Massalia (today's Marseille), claimed to have sailed around the whole island of Britain – 'as far as the ends of the world' added the geographer Strabo, who could barely credit Pytheas' descriptions of Thule and the 'solidified sea'. Pythias also reports on places 'where land properly speaking no longer exists, nor sea nor air, but a mixture of these things, like a "marine lung", in which it is said that earth and water and all things are in suspension as if this something was a link between all these elements, on which one can neither walk nor sail'. At the start of her recent mixed-media book *Time Song: Searching for Doggerland*, the novelist Julia Blackburn stands on the shore of the North Sea on a calm day and sees its surface as 'a covering of grey skin, breathing softly in and out': she was possibly observing the dead water phenomenon, which results from a layer of fresh water sitting motionless on a layer of salt water. That is why the early coastal Celtic peoples called the North Sea 'morimaru', the dead sea.

When Procopius, historian of the Roman Empire when its capital had shifted east to Byzantium, came to write about Britain in the sixth century the Roman conquest of the isles had faded into history and the isles themselves become obscure and fanciful and sundered from the historical record. Writing in the sixth century, the Byzantine historian Procopius of Caesarea had heard word of distant islands to the north of Gaul and suggested that Brittia, lying between Bretannia and the legendary Thule, was where the souls of the dead were taken for burial. This makes it a very northern, ghostly location for the Fortunate Isles. Procopius placed Brittia at no more than twenty-five miles from land, facing the mouth of the Rhine:

They imagine that the souls of the dead are transported to that island. On the coast of the continent there dwell under Frankish sovereignty, but hitherto exempt from all taxation, fishers and farmers, whose duty it is to ferry the souls over. This duty they take in turn. Those to whom it falls on any night, go to bed at dusk; at midnight they hear a knocking at their door, and muffled voices calling. Immediately they rise, go to the shore, and there see empty boats, not their own but strange ones, they go on board and seize the oars.

When the boat is under way, they perceive that she is laden choke-full, with her gunwhales hardly a finger's breadth above water. Yet they see no one, and in an hour's time they touch land, which one of their own craft would take a day and a night to do. Arrived at Brittia, the boat speedily unloads, and becomes so light that she only dips her keel in the wave. Neither on the voyage nor at landing do they see any one, but they hear a voice loudly asking each one his name and country. Women that have crossed give their husbands' names.

When Sebald, in person, or one of his characters, take the ferry from Amsterdam or Bruges to Harwich, the vessel characteristically finds itself between wind and water over unfathomed Doggerland. 'For a considerable time after he had made land, if that is the right expression,' he writes in *Austerlitz*, 'the waves were still breaking within him.' This saccadic venturing over 'the metaphysical underside of reality' might also account for the sinister depopulations that seem to afflict his favoured territories: you would hardly know from his descriptions of them that London, Paris and Brussels are metropolitan centres thronged with people and traffic. The last-named city, the place where Kurtz's 'Intended' lives as a pale, chaste, plaster character in Conrad's novella, is especially sepulchral – the 'distinctive ugliness' of Belgium being brought by Sebald into temporal relation with the merciless exploitation of its colony in the Congo. Lest we forget, Doggerland was also the sunken platform for the invention of modern capitalism, where the English and Dutch navies fought three times for maritime supremacy, and the right to make profits under the banner of Christian evangelism in the 'new' world.

The entire coastal landscape around Doggerland is itself fragile and unstable – alarmingly 'perforated'. It is an edgeland, one of the places that Sebald photographed obsessively during his long walks along the cliffs. Entire villages on the coast of East Anglia and the Wadden Sea have been engulfed in the course of history, their inhabitants swept away. Islands have vanished from the map. Time erodes, but it also preserves; and storms sometimes sweep away layers of marine silt that have hidden ancient structures in their depths. Primaeval footprints lie exposed in the blue gault clay and remain visible for only half a day until the incoming tide erases them all over again. The evidence that they ever existed is evanescent. It is difficult to think of a more appropriate symbol and setting for a work that continues the great Romantic obsession with boundaries and dissolution, with the presence and disappearance of figures in a landscape, with memory and loss adjustment. 'I suppose it is submerged memories that give to dreams their curious air of hyperreality', surmises Sebald in *The Rings of Saturn*.

Being concerned not just with space, the broad science of geography guides the imagination to a place that can only be scaled in geological time. We might call it the Cryptozoic: the epoch of hidden life.

An Englishman in Search of Robert Burns

ADRIAN MAY

England, famous for self-hatred, has an uneasy relationship with its Celtic neighbours, Wales, Ireland and Scotland. In fact, it has been said that England, language aside, is just as Celtic as elsewhere in these islands. The original Celts were European, so we might have even used this reason to stay in the EU, as many Scots voted to do. I have always liked the way the Scots were able to be themselves defiantly, in a way that seems out of reach for the English. Burns is surely part of this defiance, for a start. Burns has a night, while Shakespeare only has a day and, although shared with St George, we do not celebrate it much. It is not a night, or a Bank Holiday.

For an Englishman in the contemporary world, approaching Burns is difficult. John Cooper Clarke complains of having to share a birthday with 'that fookin' Jock' and yet is not Burns the father of all traditionalists? Is he not the first real 'peasant-poet', a songwriter, a collector of old songs and a hero to the likes of Bob Dylan, Keats and maybe all folkies and would-be popular poets? What is hidden behind the plastic Jockery and the heritage industry, the reputations, poetic and personal?

Part of the reason he is hard to approach is his ubiquity, which has rendered him somehow invisible. Scots singer Eddi Reader says 'We are all Robert's babies', in the sleeve notes to her album, *The Songs of Robert Burns* (2008) and it was hearing the delicacy and tender quality of him sung that started me seeking him. First was, some years back, hearing the late Scots songwriter Michael Marra sing 'Green Grow the Rashes, O', and live versions of this are easily found online. Next it was Burns the collector, enthusiast for and user of traditional songs that caught my attention, as he seemed to have been a pioneer of this activity, who many are indebted to, know it or not. It has been said that the Ossian poems of James Macpherson created the dream of which Burns became the reality. His invisibility, then, made him all the more intriguing for me. Arguments still surround him from other writers, especially poets. He might still be too popular to be taken seriously, or taken as a whole. But a distant tourist image can still clear quickly to discovery.

The one thing other writers agree on about Burns is his width and his ability to combine opposites. He had the aspect of traditionalism about him that combines the high and low, the rich and poor, the past and present. He makes human life bigger. W.E. Henley (in 'Life, Genius, Achievement', 1897) talks of 'the amazing compound of style and sentiment with gaiety and sympathy, of wit and tenderness with radiant humour', while Don Paterson ('Introduction' to *Robert Burns Poems*, selected by Don Paterson, 2001) speaks of 'the most remarkable linguistic resource any Scottish poet has ever had'.

What other poets disagree about is the turning of Burns to song, which he did with passionate energy, saying in a letter that he was 'absolutely crazed about it'. Paterson seems fine with this, saying his 'revitalisation of Scottish song was so pervasive that its extent can never be fully known'. For me this applies to his influence on subsequent tradition enthusiasts, while his devotion to it makes him the model for the authenticity and complex depth a traditionalist aspires to.

Paterson, though, does still insist on the 'status' and on the un-obvious nature of poetry making it different from song. Surely this is not absolutely true, as the boundaries between song and poetry are not so clear as he might like. Songs can hide their agenda too, and poems can be obvious, and some really interesting work goes on in the borders between them. I would say song is the prime medium and poems are a literary off-shoot, sometimes better and sometimes not – 'status' is somewhere else. It strikes me that poets who emphasise the difference and status of poetry are often those who have had little luck themselves with songs.

Paterson's 'Introduction' is excellent anyway, and he does add to Burns as a widely traditional figure 'still burning more fiercely than all the others' and quotes Duke Ellington on needing 'the street and the conservatoire'. Paterson also recommends, as I do, Dick Gaughan's 'Westlin' Winds', again easily found.

Sometimes a glint of his achievement comes in the most obvious and easily overlooked things about Burns. 'Auld Lang Syne' is almost invisible in its universal use, but it strikes me that this is a song about tradition. To have the world singing about the value of 'auld acquaintance' makes it the unconscious traditionalists' hymn. 'Old Long Since', as the literal translation goes, was a favourite, resonant phrase in Scots for Burns, often said in conversation. Many poets and singers had written or sung the phrase but it was not until Burns heard an old singer's version which he adopted and adapted into focus that it came alive. Is this adapting a case or more-or-less merit or talent? From a traditional viewpoint it is more, I think, and the popularity of Burns' version might be over-familiar, and hence invisible, but it is not to be ignored. There is a good live version, with an alternative tune, sung by Eddi Reader, easily found, which gives the song fresh life.

Traditional songs often speak of themselves remembering, so a successful popular traditional song about tradition is an extraordinary achievement. The English folksong from the Copper Family of Sussex, 'Spenser the Rover' speaks of the titular character with 'The thoughts of his babies lamenting their father', which urge him to return. Another song of theirs, often called 'The Wedding Song', begins, 'Come write me down ye powers above / The man that first created love', again calling on the past to justify and return to the present. Like 'Auld Lang Syne', these songs enact the traditionalist philosophy in re-membering – giving us back our lives in a survey of time and a place of reflection. Perhaps all art does this at best.

It is the largeness combined with small, telling detail that Burns does so well. The stanza about each 'auld' acquaintance buying their own drinks but taking 'a cup o kindness yet' is a metamorphosis from material independence into something larger held in the vessel of common cheer. The reminder that 'old' means familiar as well as just old seems timely. Burns's own thoughts about the song and its title remind me of Ralph Vaughan Williams' feeling when he first heard a real, old folksinger, the labourer Charles Potiphar, at Ingrave in Essex, in the early years of the twentieth century. All his fears of folksong dying out were put to rest, he reputedly said. Burns really did have everyone with him when he made the song, which might be a definition of traditional virtue.

One work universally liked, even by other poets and critics, is 'Tam o' Shanter'. This song-like poem also argues for Burns as a model for traditionalists. It is a fine example of making the most of your own world and harks back to his childhood female influences. His mother, who sang, and especially his mother's storytelling cousin Betty Davidson were sources of local folklore and Burns's psycho-geographical use of his own world was deep and exemplary. In this poem, he also shows none of the piety or humourless quality of some recent examples of that kind of work. It is a model still worth following: lots of local detail, inventiveness and a feeling of the particular in the archetype of an encounter with the dark side.

While some biographers have used the poem for Freudian reductionism, making him counter-intuitively afraid of women, they tend not to deny its power. When the dead hold the lights for the living to celebrate raw liveliness in what the drunk man sees, and all the horrors of life are on the 'holy' table, Tam's 'stomach' is not on the 'turn', however. Life somehow, however raw and frightening, seems to reassert itself in the humour and in seeing too much. Tam's cry of 'Weel done, Cutty-sark!' ('Well done, Short-shift!') is the turning point and all goes dark. It is Tam's shout of approval before all disappears, which is an approval of seeing everything at once and overcoming it with a kind of affirmative 'enormous yes', as Larkin wrote of his jazz hero Sidney Bechet. The other thing it reminds me of is Douglas Adams's 'Total Perspective Vortex' in *The Hitchhiker's Guide to the Galaxy*, where Zaphod is able to look at everything and not be thrown, where most would be driven mad.

'Tam o' Shanter' taken seriously, as comedy should be, is a version of the Dionysian Greek tragedy of *The Bacchae*. Here, the uptight King Pentheus is tempted to see the Dionysian women's wild rites. He ends up dead but Tam, like a Dionysus himself, or a trickster, evades capture by his open attitude. If you wanted more classical reference points, he might be an escaped Actaeon. However comic, Burns's breadth takes in the bigger themes.

If Burns then begins to look like our father, what are we to do, especially in darkest England? For a start there is a problem with finding readable editions of his work, as biographer Robert Crawford points out on the first page of *The Bard* (2009). Burns has his wide talent and perspective in his non-posh roots, in common with Shakespeare and Blake. My feeling is that Arden-like

editions, with glossary beside and extensive notes below, would work. I love my old four volume centenary edition of *The Poetry of Robert Burns* (1897) edited by English poet W.E. Henley (of 'England, My England' fame) and T.F. Henderson, rescued from a charity shop sale. This has ten pages of notes on 'Tam O' Shanter' and includes some tunes to the songs. On the net, robertburns.org is good, but it is not a book. So a student-centred edition, or series, like Arden or Signet, with all the information before you at once, would make a big difference. The various selections, with bits of the life and the cheap reprints with bad or no indexes do not help us take him seriously, or show us the humour and energy that reached the world.

To give credit to Burns' passionate conversion to song, the books might include a compiled album of songs, like the brilliant versions suggested here. I would volunteer to be involved. The three performers I mention are crucially all songwriters themselves and steeped in tradition and knowledge. There is an element in Burns of the clarity and simplicity of late style, sometimes indicated by the Japanese word 'shibumi'. This seems to be a concept that would be aspired to early in a traditional education and by anyone who recognises the refined lyrical strength in the older songs and singers. 'Shibumi' recognises 'Auld Lang Syne'. Poets often begin and end in song, and Burns was already there.

Every age claims Burns, it seems. The Romantics can be represented by Wordsworth's two poems at his grave and in Keats, as well as John Clare, while Modernists such as Yeats and Eliot might claim him too. Poetry, despite its wrenching and protestations of progress, is a traditional art. Before all of these, Alexander Pope, in 'The Author's Preface to the Works' (1717) says that 'all that is left to us is to recommend our productions by the imitations of the ancients'. This is how it works, he implies, despite everything.

Burns is that good, then, and he grows on you if you find a way in. Then you find that he is already part of you, part of your tradition, or all traditions, like Shakespeare. In England, there are plenty of Burns Nights. A search revealed one less than a mile from where I write, in dark Essex. The BBC website had a list of the elements you need to hold one. While these seem to be an excuse for an expensive meal at worst, at best they actually celebrate a poet, which is no mere thing. At root Burns Night is a genuine popular festival celebrating poetry.

In England, 23 April should be a Bank Holiday and we need something I might call Shaky George Night. There could be tales of and from the various St Georges and his countries; there should be bits of Shakespeare and his songs and some bits put to music (the sonnets work well). There should be strangers to bless from outside and 'see ourselves as others see us' with their own dances, stories and songs. We could have fun planning it and keeping it from the clutches of the partial, making ourselves as broad and universally local as Robert Burns himself.

We know what Burns thought of us English from his poem 'The Author's Earnest Cry and Prayer', addressed to parliament (primarily but perhaps not exclusively to 'Scotch representatives') in St James's, Westminster:

In spite o' a' the thievish kaes,   [jackdaws]
That haunt St Jamie's!
Your humble Bardie sings and prays,
While Rab his name is.

Burns 'sings and prays' for us all in these islands and we can hear him from England – even from darkest England.

Recommended listening:
Michael Marra; live 'Green Grow the Rashes'
Dick Gaughan; 'Westlin' Winds'
Eddi Reader; live 'Auld Lang Syne', with alternate tune
Ewan MacColl and Jean Redpath have recorded many songs, but my favourite album is an old LP from 1968: *William McAlpine sings Robert Burns*.

Toriano Redivivus

LISA KELLY

Last night saw this season's second Bijou Torriano poetry event, aka Tentative Tender Tendrils from the Torriano, shortened to T4, now that Heathrow has mothballed Terminal 4 until 2021 at the earliest.

Mothballed could apply to how many of us feel who are used to attending live poetry events. Little poem-shaped holes have been eaten into the fabric of our lives. Of course, I appreciate the cyber hangouts we've colonised in their place and am an active participant at launches of collections and magazines, but I miss live events: the atmosphere, anecdotes and seeing poets from the waist down.

The space I've hankered after most has been the Torriano Meeting House in Kentish Town. It has a unique history in the poetry world. In 1982, it was squatted by John Rety, Susan Johns, and their daughter Emily, until, in the 1980s, John was paid a wage to run the Meeting House. John was born in Budapest in 1930 and his life experiences – he saw his grandmother shot in front of him – led him to become a peace-loving anarchist. It wasn't necessarily the reputation of the poets, but his acerbic and often hilarious hosting that attracted audiences. John had no qualms telling poets their wares were rather shoddy, and what they might do to improve their poetic sensibilities, which often involved buying collections from his Hearing Eye imprint. He had no time for poets interested only in the sound of their own voice and would tut loudly if anyone attempted their version of an Icelandic Saga. Over the years, the Torriano has hosted both award-winning and novice poets, and the Poetry School too has its origins here.

After the heady 1980s, the 1990s brought the decimation of arts funding. Once, the Torriano had its costs covered, including £10,000 rent per annum, but it is now entirely user funded and has had to fight off plans for redevelopment along the way. Fortunately, with the onset of Covid, rates are not being charged for 2020–2021 and rents have been reduced, plus a bid for a business grant for rates payers proved successful.

The Torriano is safe – for now. Most of its Sunday night poetry audience has migrated online via Zoom during Lockdown, and indeed it has attracted new audiences from America, Ireland and Croydon. My fear is, however, that this cyber success could prove the venue's downfall if the authorities argue that since audiences are so much healthier in the unreal world, real life meetings are no longer necessary.

These fears led to my first foray into hosting T4. Emily, poet Katherine Gallagher and I went through Covid risk assessments via Zoom and decided it was worth trying. It's not easy to open up an arts venue, and I pity theatres. It takes an inordinate amount of thinking about how space is used: surfaces; signage; rubbish; eating; drinking; entering; exiting and everything in between. We decided to cut off the basement kitchen, forego the bottles of red offered at the interval and banish mingling.

On 8 September, armed with two large boxes of bleach and paper towels, I arrived at the Torriano for the first time in six months. It was strange and lovely to feel the familiar floorboards beneath my feet and smell that musty mixture of books, history and good times. There has also been a lot of red wine spilt over the years, which might explain it. Seeing the flyers on the entrance table with the names of all the poets who should have read but didn't, and all the artists that should have exhibited but couldn't felt melancholy.

It felt slightly surreal, too, setting up the chairs as if an event were about to take place, but I needed to work out the new normal capacity. I counted twenty-six chairs, three spaces on the day bed, two spaces on the trestle at the back and three white stools. A grand total of thirty-four. With my trusty social distancing measurer, going for a minimum of one metre distance with people wearing masks, I took away all superfluous chairs. Room for eight audience members tops, one host in the wicker chair in the corner, two poets on stage and that's your lot.

Then the Covid rule of six came in for Monday 14 September. So, I reduced the audience to four, with myself as host and a guest poet.

One problem: no guest poet. I mooted the idea of T4 on social media and poet Barney Ashton-Bullock got in touch. Before Covid, he was supposed to read at the Torriano from his new pamphlet, *Café Kaput*; like many poets, Barney has been denied opportunities to read and sell his book. However, finding an audience – even a small one of four – was problematic. Many people are still shielding or would rather not risk attending social events. However, the three people who got in touch and booked their place said they would come again. I won't mention the playwright who left at half time because her flatmate messaged to say she would no longer look after her kitten.

Barney was finally able to sell copies of his book and received the door fee (£5 according to pocket) now that the Torriano has its rent covered. It was lovely to have more time to hear Readers from the Chair and they shared a few poems instead of the maximum of one, imposed to prevent open-mic marathons.

Back to last night. This time, things were even more hi-tech with a contact tracing poster and QR code that I left at the entrance. The guest poet was Joe Carrick-Varty reading from his second collection, *54 questions for the man who sold a shotgun to my father*. The audience was thrilled to enjoy such an intimate reading and hear the stories behind Joe's poems. We chatted in between poems from the safety of our socially-distanced chairs and felt all the better for being together. Although I can't claim a full house, I remain committed to T4, especially as the smell of mothballs is set to linger.

Marianne Moore Buys Some Bananas
JOHN CLEGG

I work for a small bookshop on Bury Place, in the centre of London near the British Museum. From our front window you look down an alley called Gilbert Place. Two shops to the North is Bury Food and Wine, a former greengrocers where on 8 July 1911 Marianne Moore bought some bananas, 'fine fruit – the best we have had', she wrote. ('It has on all the bags, I notice, "only canary bananas sold at this establishment."') You can still buy bananas there today; I bought a bunch for Marianne Moore's sake this morning. She bought her own walking back with her mother from the British Museum underground station. This station on the Central London Railway, precursor to the Central Line, is now defunct, and roughly above its old location stands Swedenborg House, the headquarters of the Emanuel Swedenborg Society, founded to print and publish his works, a remit they have interpreted broadly. A couple of years ago, I walked round to collect some copies of a Homero Aridjis title for the bookshop; the gent on the desk led me down two flights of stairs into the deep cellar where they store the long-unsold print runs of Swedenborg, and invited me to press my ear to the curved brickwork; I heard after a while a train rush past, and that was the edge of the old British Museum Station.

Moore and her mother, during the month they spent in London on their first tour of Europe, regularly took this line. On the 8th they were returning from Hampton Court; they'd taken the Central Line to Shepherd's Bush, and then the tram to Hampton Court. (The tube took half an hour; the tram took an hour and a half.) They changed trams at Twickenham. The tramline they switched onto had been running for only eight years, since 1903, and is the reason the Twickenham High Street today is so unconscionably wide. I know this because, through the November lockdown, I've been on half-furlough; wanting to keep busy in an empty London, I've walked and biked as much of Moore's London itinerary as possible.

The Moores had taken rooms on the first floor of 22 Bedford Place, now Bedford Way. The house has been demolished; I think it was roughly on the site of the current UCL bar. At the start, their journeys sprawled West from there. They were reliant on a slightly out-of-date Baedeker guidebook – the 1908 *London and its environs* – but on 16 July, a friend they'd met on the voyage over lent them the 1910 *Scribner's Magazine Guide*, which supplied a lot of their walks from that point. (There are digitised copies of both guidebooks on archive.org.) On the 23 July, for instance, I'm pretty sure that Moore and her mother did Walk 8 from the Scribner's guide, 'Along the Strand and Fleet Street'. (My itinerary for the Moores in London is taken from letters to her brother. These are badly transcribed in the Faber *Selected Letters* – I'm going off the transcripts first printed in the *Marianne Moore Newsletter* (VI, 1–2), 1982.)

There are a handful of surprising survivals. On 13 July, Moore visited Elkin Matthews's bookshop at 6B, Vigo Street, to buy Ezra Pound's *Personae* and *Exultations*: the frontage of the shop is still there. (It's now the Burberry shop.) You can still eat plums in the green space by the Templar Church, as Moore and her mother did on July 23rd, if you like. Moore was surprised by how many English people carried their dogs over the road; crossing the Great West Road in Osterley, I saw an old lady pick up and carry a Scottie terrier who seemed perfectly capable of walking it himself. In lockdown of course the zoo is out of bounds, but I've seen the mice eating crumbs left over by the lions, and Moore saw it and appreciated it as well. And then there are those bananas from Bury Food and Wine.

But by and large Moore's London has been effaced. Some of this is just through sparsity of record: I'd be keen to find out where it was in Bloomsbury that Moore and her mother went to watch a house on fire, on the evening of 29 July, but I've had a look through the next days' newspapers and can't find any information. There are some missed connections – Virginia Woolf would move into a house in Gordon Square, round the corner from where the Moores had been staying, a month after they'd left for Paris – and some fragile possible connections; the Moores might well have passed Charlotte Mew on the pavement, who was living a few hundred metres away on Gordon Street. But in general, beside the impersonal tourist stuff, which anyway you can't get to in lockdown, most of the buildings she mentions and most of the routes she takes have been demolished.

This transience was an aspect of London which was familiar to Moore as well. Her favourite destination in London was the Battersea Bridge, to which the pair made several visits, one late at night by horse-drawn omnibus. Moore loved it because it was the subject of Whistler's *Nocturne: Blue and Gold*; the bridge itself had, of course, been replaced since Whistler's painting. Walking over Battersea Bridge myself, I thought of Moore thinking of

Whistler. The current bridge has nothing to do with the painting, just as the original bridge has nothing to do with Moore's poems; as a poet she's the exact reverse of Whistler as a painter, bright-edged and concrete where he's fuzzy and ambiguous. The other things of London which Moore loved – the policemen ('like young demi-gods holding up traffic'), the frontage of a particular club on Piccadilly, the 'Rake's Progress' at the John Soane Museum, the portrait-panel of the mummy of Artimidorus at the British Museum – are distinguished through their hard lines.

Letter from Wales

Sam Adams

For a few weeks now I have been taking a walk down the hill from our house and, via Broadwalk and the road along the Common, back up the hill. It is little more than half a mile; enough, I hope, at least to keep me mobile. There is a cluster of shops at the bottom of the hill. The small supermarket usually has a well-spaced queue when I pass by on the other side. If I am lucky, a couple of blackbirds are singing competitively part of the way, but my route is just outside the perimeter of the Roman fortress and there is nothing notable to see, far less look forward to, on my brief passage. It was then a surprise to find last Friday three or four houses in Broadwalk had bunting strung along the railings of their front gardens marking the 75th anniversary of the end of the war in Europe.

I remember the beginning of the war, 3 September 1939. At 11.15 a.m. I was with my friends George and Trefor in their house across the road that Sunday when Chamberlain made the announcement on the wireless, and a couple of months short of my fifth birthday. It was not the prime minister's words that imprinted the occasion on my memory, but the reaction of my friends' mother and father – a peculiarly penetrating silence. They also had two sons old enough to bear arms. I recall more clearly, on my way home from afternoon school, Tuesday 8 May 1945, walking down the terraced hill of Coronation Road, Gilfach Goch, seeing women in animated conversation over front garden fences and being told, 'The war's over.' That was the year I passed 'the scholarship', as the 11+ was then known (though I was ten), and was soon to embark on new friendships.

The years between five and ten, when I began to become aware of a world beyond immediate family and the valley, were dominated by the war. To me, and tens of thousands like me, it was normality. We had no remembered experience of peacetime; so far as we were concerned, there had always been talk of battles and terrible losses, always cinema newsreels of fighting, always the blackout, always rationing. When was life before we carried a gas mask in its cardboard box? Had school windows ever been other than criss-crossed with glued strips of brown paper to

mitigate shattering from bomb blast? I was three weeks past my seventh birthday when, in December 1941, news broke of the sinking of the capital ships HMS *Repulse* and *Prince of Wales* in the South China Sea and, though it did not mean much to me at the time, I saw the devastating effect it had on my parents and my sister, whose husband, a long-serving naval man, was a gunner on the *Repulse*. In due course the official letter arrived saying he was 'missing believed killed'. He is named in the list of more than forty men from the valley on the recently re-dedicated World War II Memorial in Gilfach's Welfare Park. Other families, too, were sorrowing over lost loved ones or in agonies of uncertainty over the missing.

Not long before, miners had been on the scrap-heap labelled Depression, but in September 1939 coal was again a precious commodity, vital to the war effort. It powered the ships and fuelled electricity production and the furnaces making steel for weapons. Mining became a 'reserved occupation' – that is, miners were not permitted to enlist. (A few years into the war, a tenth of young men called up for military service were drafted instead to coal mining; they were known as 'Bevin Boys', after Ernest Bevin, Minister of Labour and National Service in the coalition government.) All across South Wales, the collieries worked non-stop, three shifts a day. My father, sole electrician in 'the Squint', the colliery where he worked, and formally 'days regular', could be, and not infrequently was, called out to breakdown emergencies in the depths of night, by loud hammering on the front door. He also became a 'special constable'. I do not recall this entailed wearing a uniform or even an arm-band, or regular duties of any kind, our local police, a sergeant and a constable, both of impressive stature and demeanour, seemingly having everything under control. I suppose he was available if ever called upon, but the call never came. His un-service did provide a rare moment of hilarity in the grey days after the war when he received a commemorative medal and found from the inscription on the rim that he had been a sergeant.

Mining towns and villages were potential targets for enemy bombers, but only Cwmparc in the Rhondda suffered substantial damage and loss of life. The sound of the air raid siren was a part of everyday life, and a brick and concrete air-raid shelter for the street no more than thirty yards from our door was finally demolished only years after VE-Day. It had never been used, but there was a bomb. It fell in the early hours a few days before Christmas 1940, jettisoned by an aircraft, as I think now, limping back to an airfield somewhere in the north of France from the terrible blitz on Liverpool in which hundreds were killed, and hit the lower slope of the mountain just behind the church, where its high explosive made a crater about twenty feet deep. Although only a few hundred yards from our house, its detonation did not disturb my sleep. I heard about it at breakfast and soon joined a small crowd peering into the inverted cone of reddish clay from which wisps of smoke were still rising. Here and there in the excavated mud thrown up by the blast were shards of bomb-casing, jagged chunks of metal like lightning crystallised, still hot and heavy in the hand. For a week or two these could be traded for cigarette cards, marbles or foreign stamps with boys from the lower end of the valley who had been late reaching the site, but then interest faded. The windows of the church had all been smashed and the roof, though it still appeared sound, so damaged that the building was unsafe. It was not repaired and re-opened for twenty years. Near the church, the local GP's fine, detached house had also been badly damaged, and the doctor and his wife, still abed, had fallen through to the floor below, though whether that was from some freak of blast or another bomb, so far as I am aware, no one ever determined.

My couple of bits of shrapnel rusted on an outside windowsill and eventually disappeared. By VE-Day I had a small collection of war memorabilia, some Allied forces cap badges, a few brass cartridge cases, possibly picked up on the Home Guard firing range the other side of the valley and, the most prized, from a Nazi airman's uniform, yellow on green, a stylised eagle, wings spread, a wreathed swastika in its talons. I remember the VE-Day festivities, the buns and sandwiches, jelly and pop on trestle tables set up in the Co-op Hall, where Sunday School classes were held. And I remember the red, white and blue lights my electrician father had arranged in a large V-sign at the front of the house that blinked with such speed and ferocity men freshly emerged from the nearby Con Club after a heavy night of celebration were seen to blink and stagger. The awfulness of the war with Japan continued, but that was one down.

Much juice in air and cell
From the Journals, 21/22 July 1972
R.F. LANGLEY

At the Villa Fasola, Camera Bassa, Via di Santa Margherita a Montici, Firenze

A white sky, just blue, chinks and spots through leaves. Sprung across the window, bouncing in a warm stir of air, branches of fig, thick leaves, notched and curled carrying powder-blue lights and cabbage-green shadows, grey branches, yellow branches, pink branches, thick yellow-white stems and veins. Behind it a thick ledge, two thirds up the window space. Dark green slatted shutters open, white frames, white-squared windows open inwards, white linen curtains, thin but not shifting, white walls with grey skirting painted round, white central heating pipes, the curtains on thick wooden rings on a knobbed brown wood rod. The floor, terracotta tiles, big tiles, solid as stone, glazed texture, highly polished, right through the flat, corridor and all paled orange, cold to the feet, mixing soft shadows and reflected lights while the walls and ceiling stand matt white. Huge wardrobes of plain old brown wood in bedroom and living room. A round table, old again, with slender, nearly straight legs suddenly taking ankles and ending in tiptoes dog's feet. Cane chairs. A pair of unpolished small tables, square tops like trays with edges, and turned legs, kneed with Jacobean pyramid leg armour, on either side of a bed that is a couch, covered with blue cloth with a white flower pattern in a strip up both sides. The back of the couch a slightly puffed straw pad set up the wall. Mirrors in picture frames, big and plain wood, small, broad, heavy and gilded. A plain dark green dish on the table, chipped.

In the bedroom, darker and deeper, a step down, and sunk under beams supporting a raw red brick ceiling, as if freshly stained. Crossed cane lattice bedheads, a low pair of beds, simple white blue-striped bedcovers. Long narrow rough sheets, nothing more needed. Ornate chest of drawers with squared jutting corners and drawers that look like pairs but open as one. Crock fireplace here, also a deep recess with shelf, a room for shuttering, letting in air, not light, maturing the sweet smell.

Now outside, in the little upper garden by the bleached, crackling cane chairs and table, under a quince tree. The earthenware pots at the ends of hedges, or with new shrubs lanking in them. Wasps thump and crawl. Huge rust-red insects buzzing loud and whirring and blurring, burr through the air and into the hair. Are they cockchafers? A brimstone butterfly twists quickly over one hedge and across, pairs of small greyish-blue butterflies flicker low on the grass, twisting, landing to show the pale orange on the underside of their rear wings in a row of spots. Check on these. Many ants, the size of garden ants and the colour, but with big red heads and with abdomens heart-shaped, like tiny cocked lockets, raised and twitched. Minute ants. Wood ants on walls. A lizard ducks under the coping of a wall at the end of the garden, others, smaller, yellow and green and black, find the recesses in the wall of the road, or bask on the road itself, moving swift to cover.

What are these many flowers? Like forget-me-not or like scabious, but not quite like? Certainly scented mallow in the hot grass, growing unexpectedly in a lawn like Mediterranean daisies. Olives of course, silver of course, rather old, rather small and cool, if always gesticulating, in the lower garden. Our lawn is fruit trees, cherry I think, apple I see, ripe too, and are those plums? Quince? Certainly fig trees. Cypress, twice as tall as the house, dark shuffling gothic reminders. A pine, flat-topped, just as tall, that clear trunk and fan of branch under the dense head. The soil is yellow mud, red clay, dried in cracked plates in the watered plant pots. Leaves are paling the colour of autumn willow and falling into the grass all the time.

Beyond the garden, the city, Duomo and bell-tower to the extreme left, Bargello, Palazzo Vecchio, Santa Croce, all the time in a haze today, and beyond this, villa country, walled with breaks of black cypress, egg-yolk walls, cooked red roofs, and much juice in air and cell.

Edited by Barbara Langley, November 2020

Poems and Features

Icelandic Journal
MILES BURROWS

From Isafjord we came to Thingeyri,
The water grey as a knife,
Skuli so drunk he can't walk. But I help him.
The landlady shows me the guest book,
The names of the English nineteen-year-olds.
I see the juvenile handwriting
'God help us all! We need it!' The sketch of the boat.
She heard their voices on the radio
As the ship was going down. It still upset her. Maybe
I would take this page and give it to their parents
Back in England. I didn't look too keen
And she said it was all a long time ago
Their addresses may have changed
And anyway it was better to leave it now.

'They used to call me mother,'
Touching me lightly as she puts out more food.
The grey hulk lies still in the grey water
Like something out of an old newsreel.
Skuli says when he went to Greenland
The drinking water froze solid in the tank.
He's saving to go to University.
The snow falls dreamily in its paperweight.
The croak of a raven echoes across the fjord.
The water gleams black and purple as steel.
Icelandic humour is like the humour of Leeds.
On the snow-covered shore, a few sheep and hens.
A sheep is picking at a piece of seaweed.
No lifeboat, though there is a place for one on the deck.

On shore, a half-built swimming pool, and a graveyard.
A little grove of trees about the graves.
Christmas trees have difficulty surviving
And grow up with half a side missing.
The village is a church and two colossal oil drums.
A woman is hanging washing up to dry
With a couple of fish, in the sepia daylight.
At table, the mariners are dumb.
Pallid, silent, they have seen too much,
Done too much, had too much done to them.
Without energy to switch on the dance music
They have less to say than the ravens,
Snort at each other as if through gills
And are feasted by the grieving landlady.

They sit by the plastic roses
Speechless as if coming from a traffic accident.
She still hears the voices of the drowning
And touches us to make sure we are real.
Upstairs the bedroom rocks, buffeted by the wind.
A heavy picture of fruit, Christ knocking at the door.
In Isafjord they tried to get people to dream
With a lottery of tickets to the Canary Islands.
Bronzed people smiling in winter sunlight,
A woman sits in a huge straw sunhat
But tickets for the lottery are slow to sell.
Where the snow drops into a black sea
The ravens are large as dogs
And the sea blue-black as a six-day growth of beard.

November 4

Icicles hang from the cabin roof
Snow and ice cover the deck, the crane, the winches.
Matti the cook is like a Petersburg dandy
Twenty years old, with a velvet collar to his overcoat,
A blue shirt with scarlet buttons
And fashionable clogs with thick wooden soles.
He clops and slides these somehow over the icy deck.
Jan the skipper evades my questions
Like a surgeon dodging the patient's curiosity.
The soft je sounds recall Russian or Polish,
Some small nouns resemble antique English
Like children hiding under heavy pieces of furniture.
The distortion of a into ao like the cawing of ravens.
Under tungsten lights the snow takes on a pained
    expression.

The guest house gurgles all night, and today
The sea has the blue-black sheen of a blunt iron axe.
On the sand, the skull of some unknown creature,
And a curly ram's horn tinged with russet.
The blizzard has shut everyone in their houses
Except two boys on a tractor
And Tutti's two daughters Helga and Bjarnfrida
Playing with an old bicycle wheel and a collection of ram's
    horns.
Morning brings no daylight. The sun half rises ash pale
On the horizon to slump down in a haggard trance
Watched over by the punctual necromantic moon.
Four ravens fly over with soft treble voices,
They tumble over each other playfully
And produce dark wooden notes like a Chinese block.

The sea is looking furry, the sort of fur
That could be steel shavings. Black coffee and
    smorgasbord.
The gait of the skipper is stooped, suggesting a pit pony
That has been working too long.
Sometimes you can step on board the FRAMNES
At other times you have to pull the hawser
Inch by inch. You have to judge,
Can you pull the boat in more, or jump.
There's a crucial point where you have to decide.
That varies with the ice, alcohol, the wind, and your mood.
Skuli's drowned uncle appeared to him in a dream.
At the time he thought nothing of it.
Tutti says Oli is drunk 'up to here'
And marks a level halfway up the chest.
Skuli says my job is not too difficult:
The trucks bring tubs of coiled and baited line.
Forty of these. The crane lifts them aboard.
I lug them to the port companionway
And wedge them tightly so they don't fall over.
The tungsten lights are on and cardboard boxes
Litter the gangways. The plumber hasn't finished
Fixing the lavatory. Half the bulbs are missing
In the cabins. The intercom's not repaired.
The skipper says we may go out tonight.
On the landlady's advice ('don't tell them I told you!').

I ask about insurance. Matti wants
to cut my beard. He says it's too fierce, too 'grim'.
Under the full moon, the sea still as a cat.

A brilliant moon risen behind the mountains
In the north, holds them in crisp silhouette,
casts sparkling light onto the snowy mountains in the
    east.
Children are playing 'statues' on the icy street.
They greet me as I go by. 'Hello Madam!'
(Because I have my duffel hood pulled up)
'Going fishing without a boat? In your gumboots?'
I point to the moon. Tuli! They say Tuli!
I walk down to the quay, on edge.
A housewife watches from her window.
It's a lovely night. I go to pee in the snow.
Venus shines in the east, very near and potent, flame
    coloured.
(I think it's Venus. It could be Mars).

The ravens circling the television mast
On Sandafell bring to mind Italian paintings
Of Golgotha. But Italian paintings are hung
In an airconditioned gallery like a wine cellar
Or the shade of an Italian square. Where are the umber
    trees?
The windless sky? The stillness of the crows?
The gently receding distance? The towers? The terracotta
    roofs?
If I am to die let me be crucified
By an Italian painter on a summer evening
With a long vista of green and autumn leaves,
The sound of distant hammers, and a donkey, soldiers
In ornate helmets, a merchant passing in a rich vermilion
    cloak,
With a high collar, greyhounds, a distant hunting scene,
Pages in scarlet hats.

At Sea

We're on board. Half midnight: Tutti wakes me.
The light hurts my eyes, in the lurching room
I lever myself out of the bunk and take a wide stance.
Skuli, opposite, sleeps fully dressed. Oli still asleep.
In the galley I get one bit of white bread, butter and
    marmalade.
And one cheese biscuit with ditto. I wait for Oli and Tutti.
The gloves are dry, both pairs. I put on one pair,
Two pairs and your hands can't breathe in the diesel
    fumes.
I go aft where two tubs stand side by side.
Tutti has his long bamboo pole
With a light flashing at one end. This is a marker buoy.
Oli is ready with the anchor.
They do some complicated trick with the ropes
Like a child cutting his head off with a piece of string.
The rope seems to go through the side of the boat. I feel
    sick.

I drag the tubs. Each tub holds a line about fifty yards
Carrying baited hooks at yard intervals.
Each tub must be humped over the coaming from the
    hatch to the deck.
Skuli says to handle the tubs carefully
So I let him do most of the work. I just hump the tub
So far and let him do the rest.
Sometimes I hump it all the way. But not
If he tells me to handle them with more care.
When I hand him the tub I make a gesture
Of holding the handle as if helping him
To hoik it into place. But I don't take any weight.
It's an empty gesture, like pretending
To help a woman off with her coat.

Now Tutti comes and waters the tubs with a hose.
I resent this as it makes them heavier.
But I let him do it as if doing him a favour,
Though he is demonstrating that this is my job.
Skuli does the same and looks at me, and I let him.
Then he says, 'You should water the tubs.'
I hang the hose so the water pours into the tubs.
But he comes again and shows me, watering them
As carefully as if they were tomatoes,
To thaw the ice, so that the baited line
Won't stick to itself. I go on hefting the tubs
Over the six-inch coaming of the hatchway
And schlep them along a track to the point
Where Skuli shoves them to their final base
In pairs, where he secures the tail of one baited line
To the head of the other. I stand against a bulkhead
Clutching the rungs of a ladder. As the first line
Is thrown out it uncoils furiously
Like a rattlesnake as the boat increases speed
And bits of squid hurtle into the air and I lean back
To avoid the flying squid fragments.
I lean back into an opening
To relieve the nausea from diesel fumes.
When forty lines are out
They'll make a half mile line close to the bottom.
We put the empty tubs into a new position
On the foredeck. The task begins again.
I comfort myself there are forty tubs.

In mathematics, forty can never exceed itself.
Eight groups of five or four of ten? It makes a difference
Because each journey dragging the tubs
Over the pitching icy foredeck is a struggle.
Try five stacks of eight. Tutti has piled them up ready.
He does a lot of my work quietly. He pulls a face and asks
If I have any dreams, I sleep so much. On the foredeck by
    the winch
There's a kind of wheel which the tubs can be dragged
    past
If I can lift the wheel up without breaking it.
But the wheel is held down by a firm rubber strap.
I started banging the tubs about in a tantrum
And succeeded in breaking the iron bottom
Of one of the tubs. Skuli came
And asked if I was seasick and helped me.

First watch

Breakfast now. Coffee. Orangeade, two mugs
Rusk and butter. One biscuit. On watch at two a.m.
Alone on the bridge with the rocking stars
And smell of gloves drying. I watch the indicators.
Tutti comes and switches the light on and the stars off.
Stars on again.
A lovely night, sharp air, stars in unusual patterns
Their different intensities, some near,
Some further way, like birds calling in a wood.
I push the steering handle
To keep in view the intermittent light
Of the nearest marker buoy flashing and dipping.
Gulls floating up and down
Like motes in the eye of darkness.

Two a.m.

Waking the crew, I try to do it gently.
First the skipper Jon in his cabin
Abutting the bridge. I go in very gently
And tell him, six o'clock, so gently
That he'll not wake up for another 20 minutes.
Then down the companion ladder to the other cabins
Waking Matti and Oli, then Skuli in his cabin.
Skuli wakes as if for an emergency.
Cornflakes three helpings, iced sour cream
With sugar. I go to the hatchway and sit on the coaming
Putting on the second pair of trousers.
The others are on the foredeck. The floodlight on.
Winch and rollers and slide already in place,
The day's work is beginning.

Hauling in

'You're used to working with your soul. We work with our
    hands.'
The dead-breath: the sudden temperature-drop as when
    a ghost
Is said to appear. Maybe I slept
Or maybe this is sleep. Maybe this rusk is sleep
And I am eating sleep today in the form of rusks.
Sofa thyrnan. Sleepthorn. In the galley
The woman on the calendar is poised, chin in hand.
Above the chessboard, considering her move,
And her other hand resting on her thigh
Up which the long skirt has ridden.
As the boat tilts, she seems to swing her unclothed leg.
(The other calendar says 'Fly United',
Shows two ducks mating in mid-flight
The one in front looks back with its tongue hanging out.)

Hauling in (2)

As the lines are winched in
And each cod is pulled in on its hook
I slit its throat and sling the fish
Heavy as a young child down into the scarlet hold.
And if I pause to clap my twice gloved hands
Or sharpen the knife – am warned by a shout
Blothga fiskinn! by snub-nosed Skuli
Who unhooks them off the line
And flings them into the hold below the arc lamps.
The water runs like a trout stream over the deck
First one way then the other
And walls of water black and white
As it rises into the air, the vessel itself in mid-air for a
   moment
As if it was a racing dinghy, so that the boys
Keep their balance in the afterdeck
By hanging from bars in the roof
Then keep their spirits dancing on the foredeck
And yelling at the sea.

Sea-icicles stretch horizontal from the shrouds.
The hatches are stuck fast with sea-ice.
Ropes ice-bound, solid ice caking the mast, and hail and
   snow
Perpetually on the attack, with waves breaking over the
   bows,
And still the fish slip and slither into the hold,
The big hook through the eyes, or the baiting hook stuck
   fast
In the gaping throat, the scarlet gills
Open in a spasm under the tungsten floods.
We slit and hurl them into the hold for twelve hours.
The smell of cod is later in the clothes, in shirt cuffs,
Cod's blood in the hair, in beard and eyes,
A smell like dogfish preserved in formalin, or like wet
   dog.
A scene too brightly lit to get into the brain.
A lesson repeated too clearly, too loud, too many times,

And Iceland itself, its glass cliffs appearing high in the air
Lit by a murky orange glow on the horizon
Like a municipal incinerator, and we still five hours away
Is too much for the exhausted brain to receive
Except faintly as a towel thrown into a boxer's face.
Sleepless, inert, from twelve hours slitting cod
The one desire is sleep a thousand years
And then perhaps to wake and sleep again.
Chief memory and discomfort of those times

Was music blasting from the foremast, ear-splitting
Schubert quartets above the sea, bands, Spanish tangos
Accordion with shimmering violin accompaniment
Loud as a new mode of dental anaesthesia
That plays Niagara Falls into your ear.

Below deck, in the windowless cabin,
Issuing from the impossible-to-switch-off tannoy
Comes the sound of a seagull in an afternoon play.
We draw up the cod, self-dramatizing,
As ghosts repeat their crimes, as mad people
Are locked in repetition of their desires.
Back on shore, the guest house rises and falls,
Pitches and tosses like a sleigh
Being driven through the dark in *War and Peace.*
All the patient remembers is the anaesthetic.
As we go further North, the radio tunes
From the masthead get older
Like messages from very distant stars.
I'm jumping ship. Nobody knows, but I do.

I sing into the storm loudly
'Irene goodnight! I'll see you in my dreams!'
'You feeling better now?' Asks Skuli.
He is always thinking of me.
He lent me his gloves. The Icelanders treat me
As a not very intelligent dog
With a system of whistles and gestures.
People go to sea through lack of imagination.
'A bit better now? You did not die this time?'
I went ashore. It looked very beautiful
With the white eider duck in the water
And gulls and ravens gather
Over the fish processing plant.
The sea must love us, to treat us like this.

It is ready to say goodbye at any time.
We made fast forward and aft.
I tried to undo the frozen knot
In the nylon rope or kick it flat enough
to go through the iron ring.
Skuli had to come and untie it for me.
He jumps down into the snow on the quay
And ties the other end of the fat nylon hawser
Onto a bollard. He winds the rope into the shape of a
   bowline
Then looks at it for a while.
He must be tired, exhausted.
He has forgotten how to finish the knot.

Against Oblivion
JONATHAN E. HIRSCHFELD

Some individuals grow in significance as they recede in time. The veneration that is evident in virtually every account of Czesław Miłosz testifies to this phenomenon, so much so that writing about his portrait has been daunting.

The idea to make the portrait was born when I attended a reading at the University of California in Los Angeles in 1982. The room was packed and worshipful. Virtually all of his writing was in Polish, which most in the audience, including myself, would never know except in translation. First, he read in his native tongue, then in English. I recall sensing the paradox of a soft melodious voice that could create a feeling of great closeness while preserving a palpable distance. I knew some of his poetry and a number of his essays and recognised the unmistakable rhythm of his language. Robert Hass, his principle collaborator and translator, has described his 'fierce, hawkish, standoffish formality'. Even allowing for the animated eyes and mischievous smile, he seemed the incarnation of gravity and dignity. His large, wide face, with its strong planes, forceful jaw, and unforgettable brows, recalled a medieval wood carved saint.

No doubt it was the legend that shaped my initial impressions. His book, *The Captive Mind*, published in the early 1950s in Paris after his defection from Stalinist Poland, revealed the psychology and destiny of intellectuals complicit with the regime. *Bells in Winter* was my first encounter with his poetry, in which I learned of his concern for philosophical and spiritual matters that went far beyond politics. Yet it was his destiny to wrestle with his beliefs, and to write poetry, within earshot of some of the greatest horrors of the twentieth century. Thanks to several of those poems, Miłosz had become an iconic Christian witness to the devastation of World War II. When he was awarded the Nobel Prize for literature in 1980, almost instantly he became the voice of Solidarity, the first independent labour movement in a Soviet bloc country. Miłosz had cut a solitary path through the minefields of the twentieth century and fought against the over simplifications that inevitably followed upon the Nobel Prize. 'Out of these ashes emerged poetry which did not so much sing of outrage and grief as whisper of the guilt of the survivor.' (Brodsky). He would not be defined solely by his defection from Communist Poland.

For a celebrated writer in exile to declare 'language is the only homeland' is both a triumph and a confession of loss, and this loss fuelled his commitment to the primary importance of historical memory. Ten years prior to the collapse of the Soviet Union, from the platform afforded by the Nobel Prize, Miłosz reminded the world of the millions of forgotten victims of twentieth-century totalitarianism, as well as of the nations that remained imprisoned under communism, many decades after the end of World War II. He lamented the amnesia of 'modern illiterates' for whom 'history is present but blurred, in a state of strange confusion'. Commenting on Holocaust deniers, he warned, 'If such insanity is possible, is a complete loss of memory as a permanent state of mind improbable? And would it not present a danger more grave than genetic engineering or poisoning of the natural environment?'

During that reading at UCLA I was aware that with his Slavic features and his princely bearing he was the embodiment of a culture, which I understood only vaguely. I knew little about Poland beyond the tragedy of the Jews; however, his definition of poetry as the 'passionate pursuit of the real' resonated deeply. I understood my own task in portraiture in precisely such terms, and wondered if it had ever occurred to him that at some point he was destined to become the object of such a pursuit, even if by temperament he was a very private man. I could imagine the portrait I might make. I simply had no clue how that might come to pass.

It is said that in dreams begin responsibilities. Less than ten years later I became friends with a group of writers in Paris, which included Adam Zagajewski, a renowned Polish poet of the next generation who was close to Miłosz. Adam came to know my work and agreed to help me approach Miłosz. With no more than an

introduction from Adam, my own admiration and a heavy dose of chutzpah, I drove with my wife from Los Angeles to his home on Grizzly Peak in Berkeley in the hope of convincing Miłosz to sit for me. He was a vigorous eighty year old, and could still negotiate the winding path among magnificent trees down to his home over-looking San Francisco Bay. The greeting was friendly, and from the start I felt that he and his future wife Carole were sympathetic to the idea.

I recall showing them pictures of my portrait sculpture, and dwelling particularly on the bronze head of Eric Hoffer, the longshoreman-philosopher that I had made from life in 1979. Hoffer's classic book *The True Believer* (1951), about the psychology of mass movements, is often found on the same bookshelf as *The Captive Mind*. Their perspectives were very different, but I assumed that Hoffer, who had lived barely twenty miles away, would have been of interest to Miłosz. After being escorted by Hoffer around San Francisco in 1955, Hannah Arendt herself had written 'his kind of person is simply the best thing this country has to offer.' (1955 letter to Karl Jaspers). As it stands, the only place that the 'fastidious and aristocratic' descendant of the Polish gentry was ever to encounter the self-made, working-class, American thinker was in my studio, each silent in his own world. Some years later, when I read that Miłosz had more 'respect for hardworking lumberjacks, miners, bus drivers, bricklayers, whose mentality arouses scorn in the young' (*San Francisco Chronicle* 26/3/2006, Cynthia Haven) I felt still more strongly that an opportunity had been missed. In that first meeting, I had convinced Miłosz of my ability, but remained unsure that I would know how to engage him.

When I look at the photographs taken in his garden overlooking San Francisco Bay he appears surprisingly uncomfortable and uncooperative. I explained that this would be a collaborative effort, of a kind, and photographs would be no substitute for time spent together. He would have to sit with me for a couple of hours at a time, every day, over a period of a week or so. Usually I would expect to take at least twice that, but this already felt like a considerable imposition. When we began to consider where I might actually do my work it appeared that whatever reluctance he might have felt had been overcome. It would have to be a place close by, from where he could easily come and go, and where I could continue on my own, without disrupting his routine. His garage was at some remove from the house, at the top of the path leading to the street, behind which there was a small guest studio where I would be able to take breaks. The garage was dark, musty and encumbered, but it would have to do. They invited me to return in six months.

*

In preparation for the trip north, in the early summer of 1990, I bundled my clay, my tools, and my modelling stand into the trunk, and thought about the man on Grizzly Peak. Since that reading in Los Angeles, Miłosz had lost his first wife, Janka, and a more sustained return to Poland was now on the horizon. For most of his life no one, least of all 'the Wrong Honorable Pro-

fessor Miloz [sic], Who wrote poems in some unheard of tongue', would have imagined his future status. Except for Janka, who foresaw the Nobel Prize. What I did not know, as I anticipated the meeting ahead, was the degree of his personal torment. For many years she had struggled with a debilitating disease, and his younger son suffered from mental illness. In a personal letter to his biographer, that I only recently discovered, he wrote 'I only bow and smile like a puppet, maintain a mask, while inside me there is suffering and great distress.' This was the man whom I had first seen in Los Angeles eight years before. In his memoir, *The Year of The Hunter* (1994), he concluded his description of his wife's physical and mental deterioration with this startling, simple sentence, reminiscent of Haiku: 'The Nobel Prize, when it came, was, for her, a tragedy.'

Reverberating through the austere expanse of the San Fernando Valley as I drove north, I could almost hear his description of California as the 'elixir of alienation'. The vast American West could not have been more different from the scale of Europe, with its intimate tapestry of habitats and traditions knitted together over centuries. 'I seek shelter in these pages, but my humanistic zeal has been weakened by the mountains and the ocean, by those many moments when I have gazed upon boundless immensities with a feeling akin to nausea, the wind ravaging my little homestead of hopes and intentions' (*Visions From San Francisco Bay*).

In contrast to the grandeur of the scenery the setting for my work was almost comical in its modesty. I imagined the sculptor Houdon, face to face with his eighteenth-century luminaries, and ignoring the beaten up couch in the corner, the broken lamps and the clutter of boxes piled up on my right, I concentrated on the monumental personality before me. Miłosz sat on a high, backed bar stool draped with an old sheet, raised up on a platform I had cobbled together with materials from a local hardware store. Initially I could feel his effort, his formality and his reserve – his sense of self was palpable. Just as he had taken a stand against poetry that turned inward toward private emotions, his discretion with respect to personal matters was absolute and there was little small talk. I couldn't shake the feeling that while he was certainly there by choice, somehow I was still an intruder. I felt I had been invited to look, even to scrutinise, but perhaps not to see. There is a photo taken after I had already developed a good rough sketch in clay, which shows him good humoured, suggesting that as he gained confidence in the outcome he began to relax. But he made no comments on the process. After the first session he invited me to join him in his ritual vodka, and was disappointed to discover that I did not share his drinking habits. No doubt it would have been much better had I been able to take him up on it, but I would never have made it through the week. By temperament Miłosz was cool, and proud, but he could also display a despairing cheerfulness. When he smiled, he would pause to make sure that I was with him. If one had to pick an expression by which to remember Miłosz it would not be a smile of joy, nor even his ironic one, although I saw both. I hoped those qualities might somehow be felt in the work, as a potential.

In order to witness different aspects of his personality we needed to talk. To bore him would have been fatal. Despite the difference in age, my education was broader than he expected and this mattered to him. I knew of his struggles with French intellectuals enamoured of Stalin and had read widely among the veterans of those battles. He was not at peace with many things about the West, and the questions posed by Marxism and religion weighed on him. He didn't try to test me, but I could feel his immense culture and my own limitations. From the point of view of my task, such exchanges mattered primarily for the way they revealed his expressions, and his resistance to many facets of the modern world seemed inscribed in his features. My efforts to underscore something of my understanding of the twentieth century led to an exchange that I shall never forget. I inquired about the Polish officers massacred by the Soviets at Katyn and framed my question in such a way as to suggest a comparison between their brutality and the Nazis. Miłosz replied, in the spirit of a naturalist and a moral philos-

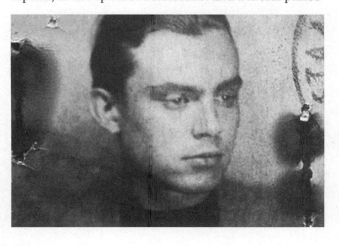

opher, that if one had a choice, a bullet in the neck would be preferable to the gas chamber. His cool lucidity, expressed not just in words, but also in his gaze, left me with a feeling that my effort to find common ground had been a betrayal of memory.

Despite this admonishment, Miłosz did not feel like a stranger. As long as I can remember I had heard English spoken with accents from Western and Eastern Europe, with intonations that I felt I could almost smell. The experience of devastation, exile and lost roots were familiar themes in my family and among my closest friends. My father, two years younger than Miłosz, had escaped Berlin in 1936. One of his first journeys after the wall came down was to East Berlin to visit the gravesite of his grandparents, and to visit sections of the city that he had not seen in over half a century. I had gone with him. My father-in-law travelled to Romania as soon as he could, in a similar spirit, and spent the last decades of his life living between a lost world reborn and the West, where he never fully adjusted. It would be presumptuous to say that I understood Miłosz, but I felt intuitively that I knew something of the forces that had shaped him. When he made a point of telling me that I was a warm man, I sensed that he was responding to this feeling, although afterward I remember wondering if there was not also a hint of irony in his comment. He knew much less about me than I knew about him, and I knew he liked to quote Heraclitus, 'that dry souls are the best…'

*

And form itself as always is a betrayal – Miłosz

I have now read about many encounters with Miłosz and many descriptions of his manner. About his remoteness, his warmth, his humour, even his shyness, his impatience, his anger, his resilience, his complexity, his doubts, the force of his words, written when no words were thought possible, his presence. My goal was a synthesis, a kind of summing up, not any one moment, and certainly nothing that one pose could possibly contain. During my time with him I watched as intently as I could, scrutinising every detail, absorbing every shifting mood, reaching for something as unachievable, as metaphysically impossible, as the quest that he himself had defined as the poet's relationship to reality. However, one must earn one's discontent. One first must notice the weight of the jaw, the extreme particularity of each feature, the breadth and slope of the forehead, the curl of the lips and the swelling of the planes, the folds around the eyes, the quality of the hair, the telling asymmetries that convey the complexity of the emotions and intellect; one must travel again and again this unique terrain until in the mind's eye, at night while the clay sleeps, one can feel the entire head as one complex mass, with a structure and a thrust, and tilt belonging to this person alone. When you have done that, you have earned the right to say that something is still missing.

Several years later I learned that Miłosz was going to be in Paris, and we spent another few hours in my studio. We shared the feeling that there were other possibilities, something less formal, and more mobile than

allied with intensity of mind, inner search married to practical resolve with which he had started out in life. I pondered the fact that something about his mouth, and also the eyes, reminded me of my Heraclitus.

The version of Miłosz I made in Paris was more than a sketch, and less than a finished work. It is filled with knotted intensity, rough, unfinished forms and the traces of accident. In 'Ars Poetica' (*Bells In Winter*) Miłosz wrote – 'The purpose of poetry is to remind us how difficult it is to remain just one person, for our house is open, there are no keys in the doors, and invisible guests come in and out at will.' – By his own account he was 'neither noble nor simple'. He had cautioned an interviewer 'Art is not a sufficient substitute for the problem of leading a moral life. I am afraid of wearing a cloak that is too big for me' (Czesław Miłosz, 1994, Interviewed by Robert Faggen). I knew there was truth in the dry, raw clay of the second version, and it felt right that it should remain just this way.

Miłosz taught that what is not written down will be forgotten. He inscribed several of his books with words of encouragement, of hope that we could continue. At the conclusion to the sittings, he said little. An empty envelope leaves me bewildered that a letter from him could possibly go missing. In the sphere of remembrance the tradition of portraiture mediates between truth and legend. Perhaps the problem was the pedestal. Perhaps, to be immortalised in this time-honoured tradition, that had lost its footing in the twentieth century along with so much else, was not for Miłosz. Fortunately, it was not up to him.

Epilogue

I never know what to expect when I invite someone into my studio for the first time. In this case the fellow was an aspiring novelist. Judging from the way he looked he came from someplace in South Asia, but he turned out to have been born and bred in England. When I told him that I liked to work with writers, he was curious. As a man in his early forties I did not imagine that he would necessarily know the ones who had sat for me, but I found him interesting, with his Sri Lankan heritage, his impeccable accent, his Buddhist inclinations and his choice to settle with his young family in France. I invited him to come by. No sooner had he crossed the threshold, when he zeroed in on the dry clay unfinished portrait commanding a corner of my crowded studio, and exclaimed, 'That's Miłosz!' In the stillness, taking a moment to absorb the effigy, he began reciting from the first Miłosz poem he had learned in high school, 'It seems I was called for this: To glorify things just because they are.'

the Berkeley version. This was the first time he would be in my environment and I was looking forward to it. My recently completed *Fragment of Heraclitus* in translucent marble was on display. The interpretation of Heraclitus was intentionally ambiguous – a deliberate play on masculine and feminine traits. Knowing his own interest in the philosopher, I was eager to share my vision. His summary reaction caught me completely unprepared. 'Why did you make him queer?' he asked bluntly, so sure he was commenting on an objective fact, without taking into account the eye of the beholder. In subsequent years this episode stayed with me. Why, I wondered, the simplistic reading?

Over the years my doubts about my portrait also lingered. When I began to write this essay I discovered a substantial collection of photographs on the Internet. When I found the photograph of the young Miłosz, it was as if I had found the tender acorn to the formidable oak that I had portrayed in Berkeley, a glimpse of the extreme sensitivity matched by strength, soulfulness

Images

- Czesław Miłosz, polychromed plaster, life size (© Hirschfeld, 1990)
- Czesław Miłosz, dry clay, life size (© Hirschfeld, 1993)
- Czesław Miłosz as a young man (© http://muzeumliteratury.pl/wp-content/uploads/2011/02/Miłosz-ML-015.jpg)
- Fragment of Heraclitus, marble & bronze, 1.2 m, Patmos, Greece (© Hirschfeld, 1994)

From Vinegar Hill
COLM TÓIBÍN

September

The first September of the pandemic,
The sky's a watercolour, white and grey,
And Pembroke Street is empty, and so is
Leeson Street. This is the time after time,
What the world will look like when the world
Is over, when people have been ushered into
Seats reserved for them in the luminous
Heavens.
        Moving towards the corner of
Upper Pembroke Street and Leeson Street,
An elderly man wears a mask; his walk is
Sprightly, his movements brisk. I catch
His watery eye for a watery moment.
Without stopping, all matter-of-fact,
He says: 'Someone told me you were dead.'

August

One more day to tease us.
I am ready by then. Cherries
Are out of season. Soon
Peaches and nectarines too.

Line of sun moving, until
Its light is all exposure, and
It is time to move indoors
But lazily, like dust in shade.

Then the warning note that sounded
When she came here. Her voice with all
The years, the sweet knowledge, but not
Enough to be prepared.

Icarus in Los Angeles

Who can say what he had in mind,
Or where he was headed,
The last man ever to walk a dog?

Water was scarce, and the sun
Burnished the paintings in the
Getty. About suffering, of course,

They were never wrong.
But none of us imagined that
Between two trucks on the 110,

I would see Icarus crawl. His
Bronzed smile and tanned legs
Hover in the mind as much else fades.

I told him about the forgiveness
Of sins, the resurrection of souls,
And life everlasting. But it was,

He said, too little too late.
Lux Aeterna; Tantum Ergo; Dies Irae.
Even the dear old hymns would not

Give light its shade, shade its dark.
People moved through their houses
Wondering where, in the name of God,

They had left their phones, their
Glasses, their e-cigarettes,
Their take on what must now unfold.

Orchard

Then there was peace in Wexford, some cars
In the distance the sole night noise.
We were moving slyly towards the trees,
Soundlessly shifting among brambles and briars.

Windows fading out into the dark
Belonged to unimagined space.
Nothing grew easily here, the gnarled
Half tended back of somewhere. When

Branches gave, she must have heard and stirred.
The wet night earth smelled rank and sour.
Sound of a lock pulled back, a key being turned.
Followed by stillness now the years have gone.

Blue Shutters

There were three shutters painted blue
And they gave on to the street
From the first floor of the long
Building. In the July afternoon, when closed,
They filled the room with shadows, unsettled
The shapes and textures, made things
Seem muted, unfinished, withheld.

From that high room, a curved stairway led
To a windowless landing. The second
Room to the right, overlooking
The courtyard, was the room where she died,
If died is not too strong a word.
We stayed with her in any case, were quiet
For a while, and then went down

And told the others what had just transpired.
I called the undertaker, shook someone's
Hand, then crept up the stairs again
To find the body covered with a sheet
To protect her, I suppose, making clear
That this was where she was, had been.
It helped to keep her private and at peace.

American Poem

Hedi thinks
I am
middle of the road.
But who
will tell
him
that today
when I had
a token
for one paperback
at McNally
Jackson
I picked
'Not Me'
by Eileen Myles?
At the register
for one second
when the assistant
looked at the
book and
then at
me
I felt like
the most cutting
edge guy
in all New York
and some of
New Jersey,
not to speak of
Connecticut,
and then –
what could I do? –
I went
back to my
road and
I lay down
right on
the broken line
with my arms
outstretched.

Consolation
ALEX WYLIE

It is time, then, for you to take a little mild and pleasant nourishment which by being absorbed into your body will prepare the way for something stronger. Let us bring to bear the persuasive powers of sweet-tongued rhetoric, powers which soon go astray from the true path unless they follow my instructions. And let us have as well Music, the maid-servant of my house, to sing us melodies of varying mood.

– Boethius, *The Consolation of Philosophy* (translated by Victor Watts)

I

Of varying mood, the tree-tops whisper-hiss their choric
    spontaneities
through my open window – a *sweet-tongued rhetoric*
    of tuneless ditties

as the wind strikes up. Melody as rhythm, and vice versa,
    the branches' subtle
disputations: philosophy's shekere, cabasa,
    the wind's rattle

of mute persuasive powers. I wonder if Boethius
    in his prison
heard through his own high window such a breathy, breathless
    diapason

as this, a desperate wind leafing through the canopies,
    and filled up.
They have no medicines to ease his pains... Quite a mouthful, this,
    of the bitter cup.

II

No squirrels today. The branches' skittering genius,
    so to speak,
in hiding, conjuring the image of a universe
    at hide and seek

with itself. A baby's peekaboo: the innocent fun
    of Brahma
in its googolplex of costumes, lost in its very own
    improvised drama.

Whatever that implies, it isn't something all of
    us can agree on,
the self as *ultima realitas*. But you forget yourself.
    Each hour an eon

of the clock, the self-winding journey; your trillionth
    step leads somewhere else
for the trillionth time, plodding the bureaucratic labyrinth
    of Kali's bowels.

III

Follow the money! as they seem to say. But what is it –
        and where can it go
from here? Nonsense verse of neoliberal diktat
        against sorrow,

the drip-drip-dripping canopy of the prison ceiling.
        Boethius'
walls were not walls, he was no prisoner. I am struggling
        to believe this.

IV

Here, on the lowest plane, sometimes you'll spot a rat's
        tentative surge
across open ground, disappearing then among the roots'
        holdings, the garbage

slumping from the bins. Summer's hot this year. The yard exudes
        a poisonous smell,
the kind that stains the throat brown for minutes afterwards
        like leaking petrol,

bites in the middle of your head like a repressed memory
        loth to come out.
For mortal beings, the underworld is temporary.
        The faint taste of rot

in warm air, fertile odours; trees muscular, overgrown;
        a nameless martyr
hanging with gross distorted face, in propria persona
        non grata.

V

I am no prisoner. Call that statement perlocutionary.
        Among such wealth
how is one not free? Your Google search *how to painlessly
        kill yourselth*

hyper-, not auto-, corrected. I float in blessing's bubble.
        The air is stuffy,
unconditioned. The window is loose-jawed, the tree-tops garble
        their philosophy.

VI

If you can't say something nice, don't say anything at all.
        Sorry, mum.
Let's start again here, try to say something original
        to end the poem

for good: something about creation and destruction
        dancing together
in endless blackout. When I ask, you speak to distraction
        of your poor mother

trudging the miles to Balzan, cradling the delicacies
        of new-born eggs
in her dress; a natural cussedness abiding curses.
        Old ideologues,

Mussolini's rhetoric, Churchill's, fading into Mintoff's,
        your body's *terra
irredenta* – what can that avail your alien griefs,
        outlandish horror?

I still see from a child's perspective. Maybe we all do
        and we always will.
Even at seventy, you're walking hand in hand to Birgu
        as a little girl

to a saint's feast, the fireworks on, in, the black water,
        skittish, mesmeric:
destruction and creation, dancing drunkenly together
        at a child's music.

Reclaiming Time
On Blackness and Landscape
JASON ALLEN-PAISANT

Why do I now want to talk about the woods? Afterall, I grew up surrounded by woodland. In Coffee Grove, the village in Jamaica in which I spent my early childhood, I was surrounded by farmland, by animals, and by the bush. Why then had I never felt this urge to stand still in the woodland, or walk placidly, contemplating it? I realised, as I express in the poem 'Walking with the Word "Tree"', that for my family, nature was functional. As farmers, my grandparents shaped the land, waited for its yields, saw their living as connected to the earth. They were not contemplators of scenery; their hands were *in* the earth. These were environmentalists without a title.

Later, at the age of five, I went to live in a town with my mother who was a school teacher. All of a sudden I was propelled into a different lifestyle. We would continue to be 'poor' but now at least we lived in a small town. We never got 'coming out of the bush' to coincide with 'upward social mobility', which became a source of frustration. Poverty can create feelings of enclosure. I believe it is, first and foremost, an affect (the absence of commodities and resources does not in itself equal poverty). We were living a half-rural, half-urban life, always with the aspiration of leaving the rural behind, because the rural was perceived to be an index of poverty. On the one hand we were trying to escape the rural, elemental lifestyle; on the other hand we couldn't afford the trappings of middle-class lifestyle. We went to the beach once a year, for example...

Now that I think about it, the whole idea of middle class in Jamaica is about turning your back on the elements. The middle-class ideal entails distancing yourself from the natural, the woodland, any space associated with the 'primitive' – and that includes folklore and myth, in which the woodland is the space of spirits, 'duppies'.

Given the attempts to distance Africans from ancestral practices, Blacks in the New World were forced to internalise a colonial epistemology of nature. The fact, for example, that African spiritual practices (including pharmacopeia and various healing practices) were viewed as suspect by the colonisers rendered more problematic an already complicated relationship to the land. The urban space is the locus of progress. Nature belongs to the rural, not the urban. Nature is disorder, 'dirt', that which drags us down. There may well be links here with nineteenth-century Europe, in which there emerged the utopia of doing without nature, of replacing soils with a kind of chemical soup, since nature, it was thought, needed to be controlled, even eliminated.

So in the small town of Porus where I lived from the age of five, people often pave over their front lawn. There is this obsession with covering the green. Modern upward mobility is concrete. The fracture that we experience between ourselves and nature, the desire and obsession to put distance between ourselves and the natural world, is rooted in slavery and colonialism. We try to distance ourselves from the 'poor condition' of living with the earth. To compound matters, violence and criminality deter us from venturing into the outdoors. Landscape and the possibilities of landscape are underpinned by socio-economic dynamics rooted in a colonial history and its afterlives. History – the past and present of social violence – make the woodland in Jamaica anything but a place of leisure. We live in a deep-seated social fracture that keeps us distanced from the natural.

The question of Blackness and landscape is a complex one. For the Black body, walking is complicated, and to walk in a dark, veiled place is seldom an innocent act. Histories of the hunted Black body form part of the collective memory of the African diaspora. If the city often proves to be a dangerous space for Black people, as recent events have demonstrated, the fact is that, in the Black imaginary, it is the city that is perceived as the site of *relative* safety, while the outdoors continue to be associated with the 'constant necessity and activity of running away, of flight', as Fred Moten puts it.

How then do we walk? How then do we inhabit leisure? What is 'nature' to us?

I am thinking about spatial enclosure. To what extent are my past experiences and feelings of enclosure rooted in colonial ideologies and histories? My current poetic project is one of writing (against) enclosure.

Allow me a slight detour away from poetry, the better to underscore the concerns I engage in my poetry. While thinking about these issues, I encountered the work of photographer Ingrid Pollard. I have been particularly interested in a series of photographs Pollard took and exhibited in the late 1980s. It is quite interesting that the issues Pollard was grappling with in the 1980s are still just as present today.

In 'Pastoral Interlude', Pollard takes familiar sites and makes them legible in new ways, playing with the viewer's sense of what seems natural or not so natural, forcing us to give attention to the ideological workings of landscape. The photographs involve 'reading' the ways that land has been marked, culturally speaking.

In the first photo, a Black woman, perhaps the artist herself, sits on a stone wall. Behind her a fence marks one boundary of a landscape of rolling hills. She is clad in white jumper, beige trousers tucked into mid-calf-height green socks; her head wrapped in a green scarf. She sits with a camera on her thigh. Her eyes look intently at something outside of the frame; whatever it is, she seems to be watching it with curiosity. The caption begins: 'It's as if the black experience is only lived within an urban environment. *I thought I liked the Lake District; where I wandered lonely as a black face in a sea of white.*'

The evocation of Wordsworth in 'I wandered lonely as a...' is, of course, evident. Through the ironic evocations of Wordsworth's iconic poem, the artist challenges the Romantic associations attached to wandering on foot through the land – leisure, relaxation, finding oneself – while highlighting the absence of bodies like her own in the landscape, and in cultural representations of the English countryside. There is an ambivalence in the speaker's feelings: the artist depicts herself as *wanting* to be there, as discovering the pleasures of the Lake District ('I thought I liked the Lake District'); and, at the same time, as feeling a strange sensation of 'unease; of dread...'. The suspension dots suggest an ongoing question, a kind of inability to fully explain why such feelings of unease exist and persist.

Wordsworth's poem speaks of rest – the rest that allows one to observe the daffodils 'fluttering and dancing in the breeze', and the rest that such an experience gives to the mind. By contrast, the body language of the woman in the photograph does not strike me as being entirely restful. Her facial expression and her legs and knees that press against each other suggest a state of tension, that she might not feel entirely safe in this environment.

In one interview, Pollard was asked whether there was any personal experience that triggered her interest in the British rural, its mythologies and overwhelming Whiteness. She replied:

> Just going on holiday. We only had a couple of holidays as a family – we didn't have that kind of income – but we went camping a couple of times. When I left my parents, I used to go with friends to the Lake District. I wouldn't see another black person for a week, and you would notice. It was hard. My white friends would be going to relax, and it would create anxiety for me. I appreciate the countryside, but it wasn't particularly relaxing. I just wanted to do something about that.

*

My forthcoming book *Thinking with Trees* considers Blackness and nature from the perspectives of time, race and class, while interrogating the cultural and geographical meanings of landscape. These poems evoke the environmental conditions underpinning Black identity, while urging us to imagine alternative futures. The book follows a Caribbean tradition of weaponising language through irony, and does so as a means of challenging social, racial and spatial boundaries. It engages a Jamaican lens on the British landscape and British ways of life, while reflecting on my changing 'identity' as I negotiate the shared and constructed space of landscape.

Thinking with Trees grapples with the fact that spatial exclusion grows into the literary field as well. In the eyes of publishers and readers, nature writing is a White concern. They bemoan the dearth, or 'non-existence', of Black nature writers. They ask, 'Where are they? Are Black writers not interested in nature and ecology?' The question is loaded with a set of assumptions and ossified ideas about nature, about Black writers, about the human being in relation to nature. It fails to acknowledge certain realities about the relationship between Blackness and landscape. It is ignorant of History, of the undemocratic aspects of landscape, and of the things that 'nature' might mean in non-White imaginaries.

*

THOSE WHO CAN AFFORD TIME

Who wanders
    lonely as a cloud
with three golden retrievers?

Not me   no   not me
I could never understand this poetry

never understand what the poem was saying
and how this could be
poetry for me

when my English teacher drilled
the imagination of a white man's country

I didn't know how but somehow I knew
this wandering was not
for me

        because
    ours was not the same kind of time
        our wandering never so accidental
so entire so free

as if nothing was coming   as if no hawk was near
as if they owned the land and the mansion on it
as if tomorrow and forever was theirs

as if they had the right to take their time
    because
everything about them was refined   was secure

    So Wordsworth's poem never made sense
I'd never stop to listen to the poems about trees
& mushrooms & odd cute things   & birds whose
    names I could never pronounce

My poetry was Tom the village deejay
It was more material   I said
    than the woods than the lives of those who loafed

& bought their time
with money   I thought
those who had all the time in the world

*

Where the relationship between Blackness, nature and history is concerned, a few observations are necessary. I will state these baldly. Firstly, in disrupting relationships with nature (dwelling practices), colonialism disrupts ways of knowing the world (knowledge practices). Secondly, the work of coloniality is based on control over nature. Thirdly, part of that control is the control of the othered (dangerous, out-of-place, to be controlled) Black body.

The assimilation of the Black to nature is central to the functioning of coloniality. But this is, of course, paradoxical, since, while the dynamics of coloniality assimilate the Black to nature, it also, at the same time, separates her or him from it. In the New World, as Sylvia Wynter points out, the African 'himself served as the *ox* for the *plough* of the plantation system which brought about the technical conquest of Nature'. The history of European colonialism in sub-Saharan Africa reveals similar logics with respect to the control of bodies and land.

Yet, in the New World, the African presence '*rehumanized Nature*, and helped to save his own humanity against the constant onslaught of the plantation system by the creation of a folklore and folk-culture'. The Africanist construal of the land as always *Earth*, the centre of a core of beliefs and attitudes, would constitute 'the central pattern which held together the social order'. Through sacred rituals (dance, drum rhythms, forms of 'earthing' through possession rites, masquerades that enacted the drama of the gods), Afro-Caribbeans created a different temporality. Thereby, they maintain a sense of the sacred, and the affirmation of ancestral ties that bind the community to Earth, enabling humanness despite social death. The results of these attempts to 'grapple with a new Nature' are well known: Haitian Vodou, Santería, Obeah, Pukkumina, the Orishas, the Shango Baptists, Rastafari, among other forms of sacred practices which sought to animate a life whose aim was to produce groundless individuals.

However, these forms of resistance, if they help to create alternative realities and perpetuate ancestral worldviews, also highlight the nature-culture fracture that begins during slavery and persists today. A part of slavery's violence was that 'the enslaved was excluded from responsibility for the land in which she lived and worked', as Malcom Ferdinand writes.

Our relationship to land, our ability to relate to Earth in a certain way determines our freedom, but also another fundamental human urge, which is the urge of belonging. Here it is worth pointing out, as Raymond Williams has done, that the etymology of 'nature' ties it to 'native' and also 'nation'...

How does a Black history of exclusion from land influence how we think about Black futures in nature and the environment?

*

I had been busy writing poems about the police and white cops killing Black people and black anger and rage and that kind of stuff. And then I realised that the time we spend pouring our souls into that kind of writing and thinking robs us of time. There is no doubt that we must continue to write about these issues; we have no choice. But I am forced to think about the relationship between coloniality, racism, humanness and time. This brings me back to my work and its central theme of time.

The observation of process is a political act linked to a reclamation of time. It highlights the fact that racism pushes us into an attitude of always reacting: to hurt, anger, provocation, exclusion. This is a theft of time, a robbery of the connection we are meant to have, as humans, with real life. In that sense, the poems in *Thinking with Trees* are an expression of my taking time, in a societal context that creates the environmental conditions that disproportionately rob Black lives of the benefits of time: leisure, relaxation, mental and physical well-being, etc.

Right now, I'm standing beneath what used to be, I imagine, an impressive tree. It is split down its bole, it is still alive, has sprouted green leaves that will be rustling way into September. But at its base and lying athwart the clearing is the severed part that looks so dead and yet so alive. The colour of brown has weathered to near-grey and the footfall of walkers has covered the wood with a layer of dust. And yet the part that has fallen among the spikenard and hungry shrubs seems so alive in its death.

> Disintegrating and flourishing
> frail and green
> The raspberries feed on its breath
> and beetles thrive in the slurry middle where the
> bole rots

Process. The wax and wane of objects, the feeling of life coming into me. The feeling of self as part of life.

Slowness. I am talking about time, a defence of time. I'm talking about the robbery of time from Black life. I am talking about the ability to be slow. I am talking about the ability of our bodies to *be here*. I'm talking about the ability of my body to be in the woods. Thinking about people, the people who find me strange because I am just standing here, the people who look at me while talking, look at me suspiciously, because I decide to stand and listen and look, because I am not going anywhere. Because I'm just standing.

I'm thinking of how we have been workers. I'm thinking of how my ancestors have been the workers, just the workers. I'm thinking of the Congo and how one man had a land almost eighty times the size of Belgium as his personal estate. I'm thinking of the cruelties of work among my people. I'm thinking of my ancestors who were enslaved. I'm thinking of rest, I'm thinking of slowness, I'm thinking about reclaiming time:

> I am talking about reclaiming what middle-
> class people call leisure.
> I realise now what I have missed all these
> years.

*

Poetry is the expression of a profound connection with life. Listening and seeing are our avenues of connection, and this is poetry's gift: that through poetry I can stop, listen, observe and participate, rather than *simply react*.

The purpose of racism is a life that is constantly reacting, being affected, being hurt, being angry. Poetry's gift is a different sense of time, not one marked by utility, accumulation, greed and blind progress – in a word, the logics of capitalist accumulation and its bourgeois ideals that produce wars, genocides, various human catastrophes. Poetry's gift to me is a sense of deep time, and that is its sense of wholeness, of connection. Poetry is a reclamation of time. Of connection, rather than reaction.

Inevitably, the poems do sometimes convey my sense of unease and uncertainty while in the veiled, hidden spaces of the woods. But they also highlight the fact that I must be there.

*

The sun splashes its light on the trees. Their exposed skins glisten. The evening glow penetrates me and I move into it. Inside me a living thing is ripening. In this month of December when night falls in early afternoon, it is a struggle to get here. And now that I see it, I am living. I was made to live. Not to schedule appointments or solve clashes on an online calendar. I was not made to spend a day in front of my computer.

There is a sadness that returns. A sadness for the boy I once was, growing up in Porus. What was my poverty? Wasn't it living in a space that was too little, not being able to go very far? The poverty of being blind to living and a slave to always doing:

> We had no time to waste
> To go far might have been just
> to enter the woods
> behind the house.
> But there was a wall separating me from it.

*

The positioning of the Black body always *outside of land*, with all its privileges in regard to leisure, well-being, health, and so on, is a key aspect of the narrativising of power and of the determinism that shapes geographies of Blackness that inscribe Black culture as always already within urbanised space, and much less within the 'outside spaces' of freedom, leisure and escape.

The consequences of the disproportionate exclusion from land (and land *as leisure*) have been powerfully demonstrated in recent times, through the inequalities revealed throughout the Covid pandemic. The issue of the pernicious effects of unequal access to land (on physical and mental health and wellbeing) have suddenly become no longer a matter of theoretical gesticulations but of vividly obvious power structures and embodied realities. While everyone was 'under lockdown', at least in theory, the access to natural space, anywhere from a backyard garden to a manorial estate, was clearly not a given for everyone. Likewise, therefore, the ability to 'cope' with the state of exception that had been created.

*

Coda

I'm really not interested in hearing any more middle-class people screaming that people shouldn't be going outside at all when your back garden is the Hundred Acre Wood.
– @SammiLouui, Twitter

Let's return to the question posed earlier: How does a history of colonialism that has weaponised land against Black lives in the Caribbean, America, Africa and Europe, how does a black history of exclusion from land, influence how we think about black futures in nature and the environment?

I propose that a Black future in nature must include an altered relationship to time.

*

I believe this can be achieved, collectively, through art. Art offers to racialised people an alternative space (a counter-analytic) to Babylon. And art for us must be togetherness, community. A way in which humanness becomes a matter of connection, again. We must form connection around the type of consciousness that frees us from the System, from the consciousness of the capitalist machinery that seeks to devour us. Can this be a point of departure for new forms of socialities for Black lives and of political awareness based on our sense of deep time? That implies the need for solidarity. And if solidarity involves connection to the more than human world, then it is also, necessarily, connection amongst ourselves.

BIBLIOGRAPHY

Ferdinand, Malcom. 2019. *Une écologie décoloniale: Penser l'écologie depuis le monde caribéen, Seuil Anthropocène*. Paris: Seuil.

Pollard, Ingrid. 2020. Ingrid Pollard on 'How She Had to Fight for Black Representation: Interview' with *Elephant Magazine*. Issue 42 (Spring). Online. https://elephant.art/ingrid-pollard-fight-black-representation-glasgow-international-womens-library-lesbian-archive-photography-rural-landscape-britishness-07022020/#.XqgFNGJm23C.twitter. Accessed 15 October 2020.

Williams, Raymond. 2015. *Keywords: A Vocabulary of Culture and Society*. New York: Oxford University Press.

Wynter, Sylvia. 2018. 'Jonkonnu in Jamaica: Topwards the Interpretation of Folk Dance as a Cultural Process.' In *We Must Learn to Sit Together and Talk About a Little Culture: Decolonizing Essays 1967–1984*, 192–243. Leeds: Peepal Tree Press.

Five Poems
TARA BERGIN

The Awakening

better

he remembered the dreams he had had
as he lay there in fever and delirium
in the last days of Lent and Eastertide
during the latter days of Lent and Easter week
during the end of Lent and Holy Week
when he dreamt of a *sickness* on the streets of Hotan
when he dreamt of a *sickness* on the streets of Moscow
when he dreamt of a *sickness* on the streets of Lahore
and saw the fabric of life unravelling
when he saw the whole world desolated

only children moving through the dreamworld
brothers fleeing from burning buildings
the older brother passing down the younger brother
the younger brother jumping from the older brother's arms
whole villages and towns
whole cities and populations
washing their hands
covering their faces

but somewhere in the back of the dream
somewhere in the back of the dream
salmon flew from their nets
falcons swam from their chains
forests of ash and sycamore
awoke from a coma in a kind of re-birth
and saw their whole lives
in a different way

The Killers

Summer and Winter:
two girls in school.
One is kind
and one is cruel.
They share the same table
and wear the same things.
If they were sisters
they would be twins.

This Rain

I painted a painting called This Rain.
All night the black ran down.
In the morning the studio floor
was a flooded plain.
Then I painted a painting called Milk River.

I painted a painting called Milk River.
All night the white ran down.
In the morning the studio floor
was a flooded plain.
Then I painted a painting called This Rain.

Mean Sea Level

Here is information about *water* everything is *water* the cities the towns the collieries *water* the cottages the mouths the denes all *water* the parks the phonebooths the towers *water* the swings the slides the pylons *water* the locks and the docks and the piers *water* the sewers the buses the golf course *water* the hamlets the farmsteads the hay barns *water* Shot Rock Liddle Stack Well Rock *water* The Snook The Winker the Training Wall *water* The Wreck The Radar The Steel Works *water* Emmanuel Goldstone Paradise *water* Skate Road Plough Road Whirl Rock *water* Crumstone Knivestone Longstone *water* Gun Rock Greenhill Shorestown *water* Leith Dunbar Eyemouth *water* Bridge Road Low Road New Road *water* everything is *water*

Quartz

Say you take a piece of quartz found on a building site on the side of a road and you put it on a sheet of paper on the windowsill on a sunny morning during the Holidays. Not yours, theirs. Say There's Nothing to Do. They say that not you. Say it's warm because of the sun yet cold in spite of it. Say your own soul is dark like the coal in the hod. Or like the soot at the foot of the coal bunker the soul no one sees but the disappointed shovel. Okay say the coal man knows but he never dwells he has raised his status where you retained yours. Say you take the magnifying glass and look through it at the quartz and say you see it shine and say it blinds the soul that bothers you pulls at your hem. Say it is a spotlight onto your good side. Say it warms your cockles and mussels and makes you put them in a barrow. Wheel them like babes by the light-filled river and sing them away. Say you're a this, say you're a that. Say the light dazzles distracts you from your own complications. Shines or blinds the self out of itself like cauterising a wound. Say cauterize. Say sear. Say Hot. Iron. Pleasing for it do be old fashioned. Today a blood blister. Tomorrow I eat from your spoon. What next, if we already share spit and injury? Say Blame. Say Hope. Say it in the cold dark of day so that your breath crystalises and I can pluck it and wear it as a Brooch. Say it: No one wears Brooches anymore.

This poem was written as a commission for BBC 3's The Verb at *Free Thinking* (2019).

Four Poems
NINA BOGIN

What Remains

Buried in weeds, dried by summer heat,
a baby hawk with perfect feathers, talons, beak.

A snail shell whose snail has left.
Under the eaves, an abandoned nest.

Bits of china in the upturned soil –
half a pink flower from the rim of a bowl.

Heart-shaped fossils for our rock collection.
Straw hats from a carefree season.

Knife blades worn to a sliver.
My grandmother's tarnished silver.

Blue bellflowers on a bamboo fan
brought back from your time in Japan.

On the mailbox of my new home,
your name still written beside my own.

Spring Cleaning

My neighbour with a rag in her hand
leans out of her upstairs window
to say hello and see how I'm faring.

I'm checking my mailbox. She's washing
her window-panes. I should do the same.
We have time on our hands, and yes,

we're both fine, on our quiet dead-end lane.
Our houses will be spotless
by the end of the quarantine –

floors waxed, front steps
scrubbed for no-one but ourselves.
The east wind has also pitched in,

sweeping the sky to an immaculate blue,
whitewashing the facades,
stirring the cherry flowers

into storms of pink.
Blackbirds sing from the tree-tops.
The light is so splendid

we could weep –
with no hope
of a miracle,

just old rags,
water and vinegar
and windows that sparkle.

Seasonal

I leave a spider in the window-corner to catch mosquitoes while I sleep,
skirt a ring of daisies when I mow the lawn.

I put out seeds and breadcrumbs for the birds to feast on,
stock beech wood in the fall to burn through the winter.

I gauge the thickness of clouds and the likelihood of storms,
track the quarter-moons' waxing and waning.

I cease to pray for the dead, I light candles for the living.

Greeting

Bonjour les morts, I murmur
as I pass the cemetery,

closed during lockdown.
Over the granite headstones,

plastic flowers whitened by the sun,
the sky is a depthless blue.

I know the dead are indifferent.
But when I think of you

who are nowhere
and everywhere,

I feel your sadness,
your regret,

as when you reached out
to stroke my hair.

Animal Spirits IV
Iain Bamforth

A hatching

The progenitor god, Protogonos or Protogenus, mentioned in the Orphic Fragments, can be conflated with the Hindu protector of life and supreme deity, Prajāpati, who has no definitive title, according to Roberto Calasso, in his singular contributions to Vedic philosophy, unless we consider it the interrogative pronoun Ka (*Who*). Both primal deities were four-headed, and Robert Graves identifies Protogonos with Phanes, who hatched double-sexed and golden-winged like Eros from the mundane egg of time and necessity. They were self-existing beings, *svayambhū*.

Who is the god worshipped by humans. The patron's name is a simple interrogation, but it loops back to the worshipper, an odd amalgam of articulated body parts and words, just like God's declaration to Moses 'I am that I am'. God's only name is his self-identity, and it is this unity that provides reason with its fundament.

A bird's life

How do birds learn to circle on the thermals of their freedom? The Persian poet Rumi knows: 'They fall, and falling, they're given wings.'

In terms of animal locomotion the unfettered flying of birds is an intensification of walking, not to speak of running, which is itself a continually averted falling.

The Russian existential philosopher Lev Shestov knew this too. 'The abyss is our element,' he wrote in his usual dramatic manner. 'Flung into it... we sprout wings.'

An alternation of flights and perchings: that was William James's definition of consciousness.

Einmal aber

In 1988, I saw Roman Polanski on stage acting solo in a mesmerising dramatisation of Kafka's *Metamorphosis* which had been choreographed by Steven Berkoff (both displaying talents I didn't know they possessed) at the Théâtre du Gymnase in Paris' tenth arrondissement. Polanski, who would have been in his fifties, looked extraordinarily boyish (he still does in his eighties). It occurs to me now that Polanski must have been working at the time on his film *Frantic*; his stage part certainly was. The stage was minimalist, with a kind of scaffolding around it to suggest the cramped condition of Gregor Samsa's bedroom, continuing with parallel lines on the floor. And the scaffolding turned out to be a climbing frame suspended over his bed upon which Polanski clambered up and over and adopted the postures of Gregor Samsa as he wakes one morning to find himself alive as an anthropod, or 'jointed legger' (Nabokov's term), but with clear memories of his former life as an ordinary human being. In the original story ('Die Verwandlung') the impossible thing happens in the first sentence, the rest of the prose being given over to working out what a rational response to such a situation might be.

Polanski's was a performance halfway between theatre and ballet, in which he adopted contorted and over-stretched postures – half-stooped, arms extended straight downwards, fists bunched, body all angles – to create an idiom that conveyed the disgust and fear sensed by the other family members, as well as Gregor's own disorientation as he moves from a sense of his hurt dignity to disgrace in full view of parents and sister. As conditions in Kafka's novella become more squalid the rejection of Gregor by his family becomes ever more complete. How do you make this obvious in a one-man show? Polanski's most effective pose wasn't a gymnastic exaggeration – and he was still fit enough to do lots of stretching and jumping – but one in which he simply lay on his belly on a beam, forearms crossed in front of him with hands dangling contrariwise so that his upper limbs appeared to form an elaborate mandible. Gregor is trying to hide inside one of the moist, dark, intimate cavities of his own body. Of course he can't. Soon, after initially being too heavy for two men to carry, he'll be 'completely flat and dry', an emptied-out cuticle so light it can be swept out with a broom. The outcome of this skin game is obvious; and we weren't allowed to look away.

What we didn't have to contemplate was the grime that Kafka makes a prominent feature of his story: the 'balls of dust and filth', made up of 'fluff and hair and bits of food', 'caught on his back and his sides' which Gregor is condemned to lie among. He pollutes himself with his own waste. He may be mobile, at least within the confines of his room, but his excreta are not. In Kafka's story, the generally abject spectacle of a creature living among the circumstantial frass and amid its own droppings (*Kot* in German) contributes to the mounting disgust felt by the other family members: a piece of vermin is living in their midst. A *bug*.

As Zadie Smith wrote in a *NYRB* review of Kafka's work, the question *Die Verwandlung* poses about Gregor Samsa's identify has become the question of everybody's identity. 'These days we all find our anterior legs flailing before us.'

A turn of the leg

If he could not enjoy the company of people who were fine and delicate, the dandy and once famous arbiter of taste Beau Brummell (1778–1840) preferred to associate with dogs and cats.

Scales of iconoclasm

'Twin colossi once stood at the centre of world trade.' So begins David Hawkes' *Ideology* (2003). But the colossi he slyly refers to aren't the twin towers that went down in New York two years before he published his book, but the Buddhas of Bamiyan, the two over-fifty-metre tall statues of Salsal ('light shines through the universe') and Shamama ('Queen Mother') which had presided over that part of the Silk Road for 1,500 years. It took several days of shelling and mining to reduce them to piles of their original sandstone, straw-mud and stucco. 'This work of destruction is not as simple as people might think,' said the Taliban Information Minister.

Colour schemes

John Keats in his letter to Richard Woodhouse on 27 October 1818, famously described himself as 'camelion Poet', someone of such negative capability that he had no self, no identity, no nature, and was 'annihilated' by the company of other people, a perverse somebody whose very nobody-ness would shock virtuous philosophers. Keats goes on: 'A Poet is the most unpoetical of any thing in existence... because he is continually... filling some other Body.'

'Chameleon' is an epithet that has been used – lazily – to describe hordes of extravagantly colourful and mutable personalities ever since, especially theatrical ones. But Keats's analogy isn't quite right, since the poet doesn't change his colours (or even shed his identity) to fit in with the surroundings, not even when they happen to be other people. Quite the reverse: his qualities are less a camouflage than a flag. They are more akin to the red bottom of the mandrill: a (sexual) sign that draws attention to itself. The poet stands out. Perhaps Keats was not so separate from 'the Wordsworthian or egotistical sublime' as he believed.

In Shakespeare's day, chameleons were thought to be animals that lived on nothing more than air. Hamlet refers to this belief, in his deliberately obtuse reply to King Claudius, when he says: 'of the chameleon's dish: I eat / the air, promised-crammed.' This is how he is faring; and the fare isn't fattening him. (The king tells Hamlet he doesn't understand a word of what he has said.)

This other kind of chameleon might seem a splendidly apposite emblem for the variable person of the 'unpoetic' poet. He shoots his hyperbolically long elastic tongue into the immaterial air, into its press of nothing, to draw sustenance into his mouth, and express its taste in meaningful sounds.

And most of the time chameleons (like poets) go about in muted colours, unless they have to do some social signalling.

Big fish

P.N. Furbank notices the desire of modernist writers to make large, synoptic works into 'water-tight wholes, Noah's arks riding out deluge and chaos', in which a single vessel is obliged to carry the secret laws determining a man's memories, a day in the life of Dublin, or all the factors working towards the collapse of the Austro-Hungarian empire. Every single detail had to be packed and stowed away in that one boat, which now lies stranded like so many other, less synoptic objects high up on the slopes of Ararat, while the river of time courses noisily and massively below.

And the Ark conceit in turn raises questions about the Deluge, when the water broke through the sky and rose from the deeps and annulled the Creation. As Northrop Frye writes, '[T]he Deluge itself is either a demonic image, in the sense of being an image of divine wrath and vengeance, or an image of salvation, depending on whether we look at it from the point of view of Noah and his family or from the point of view of everyone else.'

But as least there is 'fishing for elephants', a nice bit of involuntary wordplay in Coleridge's notebooks; his creative mishearing, as he acknowledges, of the very dull phrase 'officious for equivalents'. Then he adds: 'which as I observed at the time was a sort of *Noah's angling*, that could hardly have occurred except at the commencement of the Deluge.'

Ethics of duelling

Humans unlike some animal species have not been equipped by nature with lethal weaponry, so men had to invent the duel. Technological culture, on the other hand, has provided men with all kinds of instruments for killing, so unless the duel had been limited by ritual and custom it is likely that we would have exterminated each other long ago. The need to put even the bloodiest combats within a ritual framework seems to have been present from the beginnings of human culture. A containment, with rules and regulations. And psycho-social stakes that are higher than the physical one of wounding or even killing the opponent.

Take Silvio, the ace duelling partner in Pushkin's story 'The Shot', which describes what happens when the combatants fail to fire on each other simultaneously at 'a gentlemanly distance'. His opponent has shot first, and missed. Unnerved by the spectacle of seeing this man swallow a few cherries as he waits for him to shoot *secondo*, Silvio refuses to return fire. He cannot bring himself to kill a man who seemingly does not value his own life on the point of losing it. In his eyes, his opponent is *ignoble* (not least because he is a Count).

Pushkin based this incident on his own behaviour during one of his many duels with an officer of the Russian topographical service called Zubov. At their duel in May or June 1823, following an accusation that Zubov had cheated at cards, Pushkin showed his contempt for his opponent by arriving at the duelling site holding a hat filled with cherries, which he ate while Zubov aimed.

He missed; and embraced Pushkin, who walked off disgustedly without taking his shot.

Perhaps a man eating cherries in front of a cocked pistol *does* value his life; and affecting insouciance is one way to unsteady his adversary.

The judicious cut

Almost all the young girls in the Berlin U-Bahn were wearing fashionably torn jeans. Fashion has repeated itself in a generation, I told myself, since I remembered the same 'distressed and destroyed' look from my youth in the post-punk era. Didn't this look replicate something of the shock photographs that bad old Georges Bataille reproduced in his book *The Tears of Eros*? Those images displayed the demise of a prisoner at the hands of his executioners under the unpleasant Chinese torture of a hundred cuts or *lingchi*, and they achieved wider notoriety because of the seemingly rapturous expression on the face of the condemned man whose chest was being raked with knives.

Bataille saw 'divine ecstasy and its opposite, extreme horror' coming together and confounding this potent image of suffering.

I wondered if I ought to regard these delightful if conformist young creatures as having decided to adopt a kind of tortured uniform for their freedom to wander the streets and turn their (parents') wealth into a sign of ascetic penance, if not its actual practice. But that hypothesis loses credibility since these jeans can actually be bought off the peg with 'knee and thigh rips' and don't even need to be razored by the wearer.

Kafka, grandson of a fleischer, talks somewhere in his diaries about the philosopher Blaise Pascal cutting himself to bits with 'wonderful knives' while maintaining 'the calm of a butcher'.

Flying fish

Friedrich Nietzsche inverts the elements with the strange but striking image in *Also Sprach Zarathustra* of the man fishing on the mountain tops. 'Has a man ever caught fish on high mountains?'

Well, the irritable Poseidon was an earth god too, generator of equine sons and god of earthquakes, which he caused by smiting the earth with his trident – and a mountain can have eyes (lakes), as Nietzsche himself said, navigating the Swiss mountains like Deucalion with his mobile chest of drawers.

Liebespfeil

Kafka's stories and novels evince a peculiar and recurrent literary interest in stab wounds, invertebrate life and sexuality. He would have been fascinated by the way in which all three themes come together in the tactile courtship rituals of ordinary land snails of the genus *Helix*; the conflicts built into the nature of the gender opposition economy (which dominates the animal kingdom) occurs as a form of traumatic injury in those rare species – such as snail – that are hermaphroditic. They are creatures with a male and a female component in the same body.

During the courtship ritual, which can last several hours, each snail (and the phenomenon occurs in other gastropods too) projects a sharp chitin harpoon (or *gypsobelum*) through the body wall of its mating partner: these 'love darts' are produced in mature animals after their first episode of mating, and released by hydraulic pressure in the dart sac of the genital pore, close to one of its tentacles. Dart extrusion is triggered by fondling of the genital pore, usually after each snail has extensively investigated the other's body. Because the two contiguous snails are essentially unsighted this event is more of a stabbing than a shooting; the extruded dart can actually pierce the head or lodge in the internal organs of the other snail. After both snails have released their darts, they go on to copulate and exchange sperm, being both donor and recipient.

While the ancient Greeks were excellent naturalists, and may even have derived the popular notion of arrows fired by the love-god Eros (better known as his Roman avatar Cupid) from this singular instance of snail behaviour, it is important to appreciate that the gypsobelum is not a penile stylet to transfer sperm, as in some other species, or even a means of delivering ionic calcium or sexual 'stimulus' as was previously thought. Its function is to allow improved sperm survival rates in the reproductive partner. A hormone present in the mucus sheath of the gypsobelum, which usually pierces a highly vascular area, provokes restructuring of the sperm storage area of the stabbed snail: more sperm can be received and fewer fertilised eggs are digested in its gynopore. Recipients also subsequently tend to mate less often with other snails. The love dart could therefore be considered an accessory apparatus for sperm survival.

The manifold

Perhaps the modern way to understand the Genesis story is to realise that humans exchanged circumscription and limitation in space (namely their confinement to the Garden of Eden) for the more meaningful notion of nomadic lives that would instead be restrained and limited in time.

Except that there is no common frame of reference, and it would no longer make sense to speak of anyone observing the hypersurface of the present as having a *location*.

Rayfish

The ancient lineage of the skate, a flat cartilaginous fish with large pectoral fins, whip-like tail and mouth on the underside of its body that allows it to grind up bottom-feeding crustaceans, has been a common presence in still life paintings from Chardin through Boudin, Ensor and Soutine, to the Scottish artists John Bellany and Ken Currie, in his 'Tragic Forms I–V'. The eldritch ventral appearance of the skate, with its characteristic nares resembling eyes, gill slits and mouth makes it a discomfortingly humanoid figure for meditating on what human nature shares with the hidden and monstrous. Every depicted skate has fought in a larger space for air, and died.

Eating and watching

The two birds, Jiva and Isvara, each cognisant of the other, both manifestations of Brahman, perch on the same tree in the Upanishads. One eats the sweet fruits of the tree while the other looks on.

Nature worship

The new French revolutionary calendar was created by a commission of savants and presented to the National Convention in October 1793. The poet and playwright Fabre d'Églantine assisted by the chief gardener at the Jardin des Plantes in the grounds of the Natural History Museum devised the names of the months, starting from the autumn equinox: Vendémiaire, Brumaire, Frimaire; Nivôse, Pluviôse, Ventôse; Germinal, Floréal, Prairial; Messidor, Thermidor, Fructidor. They are, in their adoration of the agricultural round, rather lovely names.

In no time at all a wit in the United Kingdom had supplied English approximations to counter such high-minded gallic expressions of the natural cycle: Wheezy, Sneezy and Freezy; Slippy, Drippy and Nippy; Showery, Flowery and Bowery; Hoppy, Croppy and Poppy.

Slave labour

In Sumerian and Babylonian literature, it is taken as given that the function of the human race is to serve the gods by providing them with food and drink on every day of the year. Their creation story had figurines of clay being mixed with the blood of a slain god in order to create the initial seven human pairs, from which the subsequent generations multiplied. But that was before the gods had worked out the problem of how to limit infinite human expansion (disease and famine were trialled with only partial success); Enlil convened the gods who decided to send a flood to wipe out the human race.

Enlil thought he would be able to sleep again at night without being disturbed by the din of humans. But clearly he and the other gods hadn't thought about what would happen to them when the bread supply was extinguished. Only Enki was bold enough to discuss the matter with the wall of the hut in which his favourite lived (thus upholding his oath not to reveal the plan to the humans). This man – Uta-napishtim or 'the man who found life' – was the conduit allowing the human race a second chance and, in so doing, kept the gods alive.

Voice-body

The larynx (windpipe) is phylogenetically ages older than the cortex or even the muscle structures responsible for articulation and language. How strange then that the human organism which, like that of all other animals has to swallow its nutrients after taking them into the body through the mouth, is obliged to use the same aerodigestive tract for what is the least important function for immediate survival: *phonation*. There is no more intense experience for humans than the sense of implicated touch brought about by hearing other humans speak. Bright sounds are made in the vestibule of the mouth, where the tongue disciplines the teeth and palate, whereas eerie, rough, crepuscular sounds emerge from the throat and are readily associated with anger and animality.

Water studies

Leonardo da Vinci was fascinated by water all his life, devoting his attention to its properties more than to any other aspect of the material world that interested him, and there were (as we know) many things that caught his interest. As a young man, he even planned to write a treatise on water, and he talked of this work throughout his life without ever planning how he was going to conceptualise it.

Besides the scattered entries in his Notebook on the nature of water, and the related entries on hydraulics and canalisation, he left hundreds of drawings of water in motion – cataracts, currents, flumes, vortices – that confirm the central place it occupied in his thinking. Water was incompressibly heavy, but also fleet and mercurial – qualities that relate it to sleep and dreams. And time. Water was the most dynamic element, rising as vapour, falling as rain and sleet, patiently and inexorably seeking its level in all circumstances, gnawing at barriers with animal dedication. As a young man, he had observed the Arno flood its banks and cause devastation in the neighbouring farms and villages (not least at one called Vinci): he seemed to have a lifelong fear of floods and watery cataclysms – 'the inconceivable and pitiless havoc against which no human resource avails'. The set of 'Deluge Drawings' in the Windsor collection suggest his apocalypse was always going to be an elemental flux. He drew analogies between movements of air and water, and even considered water 'the vehicle of nature' ('vetturale di natura'), believing it to circulate around the globe much as blood courses through the vessels of the human body. This is the old notion of humans as a lesser world or microcosm. Some of his studies of water passing obstacles show it braiding like hair, and his pen-and-ink study of a stream of water falling into still water, c.1508–09, offers a beautiful illustration of vortices and turbulence. It is full of animated detail and impetuous force. 'It is not possible that dead water should be the cause of movement either of itself or of anything else.'

In one paper, he tried to express its characteristics, and was carried away on a spill of wreckage, nouns and adjectives tumbling over each other: 'circulation, revolution, rotation, turning, repercussing, submerging, surging, declination, elevation, depression, consummation, percussion, destruction [...]'. Sixty-four terms in all, as his biographer Martin Kemp reveals.

An obscure Japanese graphic artist from the Meiji period called Mori Yuzan (1869–1917) seems to have felt the same awe at water's primal force, since he put together a compendium of hydrological harmonics: *Hamonshu: A Japanese Book of Wave and Ripple Designs* (1903). In its three volumes every aspect of water patterns has been rendered in exquisite ink drawings – flow and ebb, spiral and rotary movements, interlacings and bifurcations, even the aerial gobbets of foam and spindrift. 'Could we not think of drawings,' John Berger asked in *Berger on Drawing*, 'as eddies on the surface of the stream of time?' No better place to see time's hard tenancy in winter or its melting yield in spring than in the very substance that supplies the master metaphor for all 'streaming'. Waves are portrayed in free form or radically stylised, and these stylisations include ribbon-patterns that oxbow harmoniously over several pages or instead break into tiny intricate semiotic details that show foam budding like cherry blossom. *Hamonshu* was intended as a catalogue or resource guide for craftsmen, who were to find in its pages motifs and emblems ready for transfer to ceramics, textiles, lacquerware and religious objects. It is now considered a design classic.

Leonardo would immediately have grasped the connection between a wave caught on the break and the glint of light on a piece of sword furniture. The associative manner in which his imagination worked was itself fluid.

Two cohorts

Madame de Staël in *De l'Allemagne* offers a helpful distinction between two forms of stupidity: '*La bêtise* and *la sottise* differ essentially in this, that *bêtes* submit willingly to nature and *sots* always delight in the idea that they dominate society.'

Pillow books

Garments are especially important in the *Epic of Gilgamesh*: they are cleansed in Tablet XI and Shamhat first spreads her dress so that 'the savage man' Enkidu could lie on her and take her sex, and then shares her piece of cloth with him, now sexualised and humanised, before introducing him to society in the city of Uruk. These of course are the first clothes Enkidu has ever worn. As Paul Valéry observed, not thinking of *Gilgamesh*: 'stark naked thoughts and feelings are weak as naked men. So they have to be clothed.'

In the course of the epic Shamhat's garment has been successively seductive adornment, a pillow for lovers and finally a form of modesty: the coupling scene is not just about the heat of sexual passion but opens on a wider experience of sexuality, for Shamhat and Enkidu spend an entire week together according to the epic, a week that takes him away from the animals – indeed makes him strange to them, for they will no longer consort with him – and turns him into a full human. Drinking beer and eating bread will follow next, both achievements of human civilisation.

Centuries later, Boris Pasternak will evoke the importance of getting clothes off, especially when they're wet. In his love poem 'Wild Vines', a couple seeks shelter from the rain beneath a willow. Like the ivy twined around the willow, the man's hands have found their way to the woman's breasts, and the poet exclaims: 'Not ivy, but the hair of Dionysus / hangs from these willows. What am I do?'

The answer is clear. 'Throw the raincoat under us!'

Exit, pursued by a bear

'History is direction,' runs Oswald Spengler's gnomic saying, 'but Nature is extension – ergo, everyone gets eaten by a bear.' Only in a Werner Herzog movie.

Burrs

TOGARA MUZANENHAMO AND RORY WATERMAN

We are turning into ghosts here. The days mirror each other.
Silence sits flat like a stone on the horizon. Muting everything.
The house is cold and dark and quiet as a cave. My daughter
wakes up much later than usual. And as I am seated, writing
this to you, she's still in bed – her body clock adjusted three
weeks back. After schools closed, she was so happy to be free

from the early morning rush – dressing as she ate breakfast,
the neighbours' dogs barking and cars revving and speeding out
of wrought iron gates, traffic flooding streets as the sun cast
its eye through the kitchen window where my wife would shout
For Christ's sake we're going to be late. Faucets running.
Keys lost then found. Doors slamming. The general chaos of leaving.

All these things my daughter now comments on with a hint
of regret. Though she's happy to go to bed late and wake up late –
though she's adjusted to the quiet – there's just one complaint
that constantly drags at her heels like an invisible weight. Eight
year olds, she insists, should get out and play with their friends.
She's also beginning to tire of asking when all of this will end.

I leave for my mother's, fleet through ghost suburbs and into
my plotted and pieced homeland. And, yes, 'When will this end?'
she says, gesturing a happy hug across her yard. Then 'Let's go!'
and I follow her command, her boots, round the fields, the bends
in countless hedges, on a route she's treaded daily, from budding
hawthorn to bulging haws, stopping to 'gosh!' at anything

that moves, or to lift her binoculars, often frantically missing
whatever it was: a kestrel trembling on cloud, a green woodpecker
fanning back to the copse. She wants to show me something.
This is why I am here: love without touch, to risk her health for
our health . The hay is baled, our calves pimpled with burdock burrs.
And, worlds away, riots have broken out again, I tell her,

slipping my bastard phone away, sorry , as silently we decide
not to navigate what we think, even for one another. We're
on the edge of the woods now, near a stable, derelict beside
a brick-strewn, dimpled lawn that was a country house. 'Not far'
she says, proud, then grabs for my hand as she misjudges
a style, retracts in a blink, tumbles hard to the mud.

Driven by necessity, we pack up and head out to the farm.
The road's a wide ribbon of tar with a cautious stream of cars.
Silence still reigns. The morning sun falls across my forearm.
The passenger seat is empty, my daughter in the back, her tears
long dried after refusing to wear the mask – eyes fixed to the screen
of her tablet. In a calm voice, she says she's never seen

so many men with guns as we drive away from the first of three
checkpoints. The city falls back with its suburbs and townships –
farmland expanding in dry blond swathes of grass where barley
and wheat once stood in stiff green regiments with faint slips
of mist layered above needled awns. Hard to imagine after two
decades, wild grasslands knotted with cockle burrs. Equally hard to

grasp how the months to come will ultimately define an age
within this century. And at the final checkpoint I hand over my pass
and the soldier's eye lifts from the document's final page –
then commands I roll the car's rear window down and the glass
sinks to reveal a child wrapped in a duvet, masked and quiet.
His eye falls cold on her not fearing the virus, but the coming riots.

But she rights herself, quietly, still fit enough, and on we go. And
we are not to talk about it – I know that. But eventually she talks
around it: 'I'm getting old now. I want to enjoy life while I can' –
and is this it? – as she leads me along a fence by a wood. We walk
in single file through tendrilled nettles, to where an unclipped strand
of fence wire bellies towards the turf. She doesn't try for my hand

this time – and makes it. The treetops ride the breeze a little
but everything is stillness down here. A shotgun cartridge cracks
beneath her toe, a blackbird hops from a stump to scuff leaflitter.
And she peers long-range like a squirrel, grass-stained back
to me, then points: 'This way'. And as we go, I tell her about you,
this poem. After all, she always wants to know the things I do,

so let's try that. 'Zimbabwe! What's it like there?' she says, placing
'there' in a mental map of a region she's traversed much more
extensively, but I know what she means, what this now means. We face
sculpted rock I recognise from childhood, that we must have come for,
but I won't say I've been here. 'Few cases anywhere until June. Parts
are now on the usual curve.' I cast a stone. It sails like a line on a chart .

The midday sun is warm and pale shadows stain the earth at our
heels. This is the good air – the air away from the city. The view
from the homestead is nothing but rhodes grass rolling out the hour-
long walk to the neighbour's – well, the last neighbour we knew.
My daughter immediately rips off her mask, kicks off her shoes
and runs through the rose garden for the swing, heels and toes

in full momentum even before I begin to unpack the car. Yes.
This is the good air – rinsed, cleansed of everything but the chain
of the swing slightly creaking above a lone dove's call – the ease
of breath reassured with the next intake that comes easier again
and again – until breathing is forgotten and the senses accept
each sensory gift given back to something within that slept

with fear – only to reawaken and shudder, blistered with emotion.
As I stand there immersed in this, the front door of the farmhouse
opens and my mother appears in the jamb. And it's not caution
that roots us in place. The mandated distance is a comfortable excuse
as we greet each other from afar. She steps back into the shadows
of the corridor. I lift the bags and enter and my daughter follows,

and we find our room as we left it months ago – the mirror above
the dresser hazed with dust, the curtains closed. Evening passes
with a sharp dry wind. And as dawn approaches, the corrugated roof
stiffens with frost and creaks. My daughter is fast asleep as I dress.
Stepping out, I check my phone. The air is cold. The sky bruised blue.
From my palm I read the morning news. Harare Under Curfew.

We gawp into the puzzle of a limestone lime-green fountain,
a lead pipe stub in its bowl, a handful of dirt. Webs of ivy follow
its contours still. And, over there, the old rope swing. I'll try it again –
but who is this now, emerging from the leaf-waving shadows?
'Are you lost? You can't be here,' he says, pointing at the new farmhouse
we hadn't noticed: bright brick over privet. Stiffly, he guides us out.

And as we trudge on home I check my phone again, see your email.
Harare's a ghost town, I tell her. Patrolled. Silent. Under curfew.
Shouldn't I have known? But our news is our news. America's as well.
On the landing page this morning: another daubed, dented statue.
Crowds facing off somewhere. Burned lots. BLM. Back the Blue.
All foreign round here. A kestrel twitches, dips behind some bales –

too quick. Then we're back. She gestures another hug. I gesture one too,
and slip into gear and out of her little lane, checking for her arm
in the mirror, lifting mine, sighing. Hoping to have done no harm.

Three Poems
CAMILLE RALPHS

Cadae on inner and outer space

Though, on the
face
of it, all space

is

is a ghost-writer
of time and thick, graceless images,
we've it
to thank for thought's remit:

without distances,

differences,
there's no will or would;
but then, who knows if a splatter
of the original, dark matter
might be better, or as good?

Mandanila Ragale on Hampi, India, once the world's largest settlement

If monkeys
march arch-
itraves,
sweat in wet

sherbet sun;
if the rubble,
red concentric
stubble, stone

chariots
and ziggurats
don't move
but the Tung-

habadra does,
has time won?
Made: known:
done; un-, un-, un-.

Rondel on Oradour-sur-Glane, France, destroyed 10 June 1944

Where the entrance reads 'Souviens-Toi'
or 'remember', the rootless grass forgets,
prickling under the brute silhouettes
of brick, the oxblood chassis of a car.

The telegraph poles carry nothing afar
and the mute wires' shadows hang over like debts
where the entrance reads 'Souviens-Toi'
or 'remember'. The rootless grass forgets

the church parameters in flames; the char
of indistinguishable bones; the sweats
of buckets, hoops and prams, and the hot rosettes
of manmade and inhuman fires – some war –
where the entrance reads 'Souviens-Toi'.

Pilgrim Suite
JOHN ROBERT LEE

1.

who will come to the red gate with the red mail tinbox
its pillars topped with red pyramids
who will walk past the yellow hydrant
and stare through the closed gate
at the thick variety of garden
wrought-iron barricade round the verandah
who will see the green banana leaf
peering over the grey wall
for who might come through the red gate on Pelham Street?

2.

*'If I feel the night
move to disclosures or crescendos,
it's only because I'm famished
for meaning.' – Li-Young Lee*

persistent lament of wood-doves
who, who has gone, gone forever?

orange wafer of sun settling to horizon's eclipse

evenings shuddering with unrequited affections

I would love you with ardent hunger
beyond your name, your ancient eyes, sensual lips
tattoo on your left breast
the inexorable news of your dying

in this hour
in which I love you
I am a poem without a theme
without a clear image of you
a line to follow
a procession of remembrances to metaphor
no half-rhyme rhythms to match ambiguity

going past your old house near the Baptist chapel

and Chinese grocery
the blue estate-wall on my left with its crimson border
trees behind it raucous with afternoon parrots
a cock under the avocado tree crowing for some epiphany
wanting a Creole love song from Philip Martelly and Kassav
to make me recall your sensuous hips
incomprehensible smile perfect mouth
your various infidelities
like the turning familiar corner into which I bend my eyes
alert for unwelcome surprises

how can I love you without you

these November days close with apocalyptic cloudbursts over
    darkening horizons

who, who has gone, gone forever
wood-doves lament persistently.

3.

'for he looked for a city which has
foundations.' – (Hebrews 11:10)

how can the last way out
not be a dirt-track
moving under a canopy of trees
their dark barks turning white
green foliage bowing over your passing
and somewhere in all that good bush
angels stroll, you are sure, fluting like ground-doves
their wings breezing above like casuarinas
near the beach-stone edge of Pigeon Island –
you gave me this Bible-text card
with that dirt-track road
between green trees
and their whitening barks
when we met in the City of Palms
in that city of refuge, city of priests
and beyond my chaste prayers
my chastening desire
you pressed my hand to your lips
and left it there
all these kind years –
I have kept it in my Book of Offices
all your faithful hours
all this becoming, as they say, one flesh
and it is, I think
a true sighting
on that sacred card with its scripture text
of the last road I want to walk with you
the road that goes my love
to the City of Holy
angels fluting like wood-doves
down the last dirt-track of Earth
beside the grace-filled trees
and their whitening barks.

4.

those who know such things
say our spiral galaxy, planets and further quasars,
the space-time continuum on which they curve orbits
are expanding fast, away from themselves
into some blue-black vacuum of solitary, dark matter –

like those cosmological stars
seems we are speeding away from each other
little time for intimacy of love's spaces
distracted by widening ellipses of the settled familiar
falling off into dark holes of self-centred universes –

there is a Heaven in which we speed towards each other
through infinite expanses of Spirit
dancing to holy nebulae carrying our names,
to enter welcoming celestial bodies
and an everlasting, ever-extending consummation.

5.

strange old rubble wall
coming through the wet window of the airport bus:
different-shaded, different-sized stones
from sidewalk up to some indeterminate,
abstract, unfinished, uneven top,
looks blackened, as though burned,
and then, more even clay bricks finish the wall
which holds rust and red metal doors –
the humans of Port of Spain
walking past it, the traffic lights and pedestrian crossing
might know who the strange wall is and its story,
is it historical artefact, crumbling edifice forgotten by the council
an unknown artisan's work...
but it raining, the bus moving slowly in traffic
we look at bridges, torrential canals, white mosques,
bars and billboards cruising under drizzle,
the young people singing Chronixx, and
a category 5 hurricane beating up the Atlantic.

'Out of the Deep Freeze'
Literature from The Other Europe

DAVID HERMAN

The last twenty-five years have seen a revolution in publishing in Britain and America. A door has been flung open and we have discovered a whole generation of great European writers from the mid-twentieth century. Writers like Stefan Zweig and Joseph Roth, Vasily Grossman and Isaac Babel have been republished and retranslated. Writers like Antal Szerb, Mihail Sebastian and Josef Czapski have been translated for the first time. Biographies have appeared, their letters and diaries have been translated and edited. The centre of gravity of modern European literature has suddenly started to shift.

This story falls into two halves. First, there is the rediscovery of Soviet writers and second, of writers from central and east Europe. It's not as if some of the great Soviet writers were unknown before. Lionel Trilling was writing about Babel's *Red Cavalry* in the 1950s. He wrote an introduction to Babel's *Collected Stories* in 1955, the first post-war republication of Babel's work in any language. Trilling began by describing how he first read Babel in 1929, when *Red Cavalry* was first translated into English.

It wasn't just Trilling. There were essays on Babel by a number of American critics in the 1950s and '60s including Irving Howe and Steven Marcus. 'No Soviet writer,' wrote Alex Abramovich in *Slate* in 2001:

> has meant so much to so many Americans: Ernest Hemingway read the first translation of Babel's stories and turned green over his sentences. Raymond Carver cited Babel as a formative influence. Philip Roth's alter ego, Nathan Zuckerman, called himself a 'New World cousin in the Babel clan' – a sentiment shared by Cynthia Ozick and Saul Bellow. Francine Prose recalls learning the 'extraordinary importance of compression, simplicity, bravery, and never underestimating the intelligence of the reader' at Babel's feet. Lionel Trilling, Irving Howe, and John Berryman wrote brilliant essays about him.
>
> (Alex Abramovich, 'Towering Babel', *Slate*, 29/10/2001)

For many years our image of Soviet literature was dominated by Babel's *Red Cavalry*, Pasternak and Solzhenitsyn, the memoirs of Nadezhda Mandelstam and Yevgenia Ginzburg, and the poems of Akhmatova and Tsvetaeva. All great writers who received great acclaim.

What has happened in the last twenty years, however, is that there has been a dramatic changing of the guard. Writers like Grossman, Lev Ozerov and Shalamov have been added to the canon.

In 1995 Yale University Press brought out their brilliant edition of Babel's *1920 Diary*, the notebooks which were the basis for *Red Cavalry*. If anything, *1920 Diary* is the equal of *Red Cavalry*, even darker, more violent, more open about the brutal antisemitism of the Cossacks and the tragic situation of Jews in countless small villages in what the historian, Timothy Snyder, has called the *Bloodlands*.

In 2002 Norton translated *The Complete Works of Isaac Babel*, complete with two essays by his daughter Nathalie Babel, a detailed chronology by Gregory Frieden and an introduction by Cynthia Ozick. In 2009 A Norton Critical Edition of *Isaac Babel's Selected Writings* appeared and more recently Pushkin Press have published Boris Dralyuk's new translations of *Red Cavalry* (2014) and *Odessa Stories* (2016).

These new translations of Babel and a wealth of secondary literature have transformed his reputation. They were reviewed by leading writers and critics from David Remnick, later editor of *The New Yorker*, and John Updike to specialists like Steven J. Zipperstein, Rachel Polonsky and Robert Chandler. Babel has now re-emerged as one of the great writers of the twentieth century.

There was an even more dramatic change in the reputation of Vasily Grossman. Grossman's *The People Immortal* and *Kolchugin's Youth* were already translated into English during the 1940s but these couldn't have prepared anyone for the genius of *Life and Fate*, *Everything Flows*, *Stalingrad* and the stories and essays in *The Road*, all translated by Robert and Elizabeth Chandler. Both *Life and Fate* and *Stalingrad* have been dramatised on Radio 4 with all-star casts including Kenneth Branagh, Harriet Walter and David Tennant. It is not just Grossman's fiction that has been translated. Antony Beevor and Luba Vinogradova edited and translated, *A Writer at War: Vasily Grossman with the Red Army, 1941–1945* (2005), MacLehose Press translated Grossman's *Armenian Sketchbook* (2012) and there have been two major biographies as well.

Once neglected, Grossman is now regarded as the greatest chronicler of Stalinism, one of the great war novelists and reporters and one of the first literary witnesses of the Holocaust. 'Grossman,' wrote the Garrards in their biography, 'was and is the great teller of truths about the war, and about its most epic battle as well as its darkest secrets.' Martin Amis called Grossman, 'the Tolstoy of the USSR.' The historian, Niall Ferguson, called *Stalingrad*, 'World War II's *War and Peace*.'

Babel and Grossman are not the only great Soviet writers to have entered the mainstream in the English-speaking world. There are new translations of Shalamov's *Kolyma Tales*, his account of the Gulag. Penguin Classics brought out *Kolyma Tales* in 1994 and, more recently, NYRB Classics have translated *Kolyma Stories* (2018) and *Sketches of the Criminal World: Further Kolyma*

Stories (2020). Shalamov spent almost twenty years in Stalin's labour camps. Solzhenitsyn wrote that after first reading Shalamov's poems in *samizdat* in 1956, he 'trembled, as if from meeting a brother'. He invited Shalamov to collaborate with him on *The Gulag Archipelago*.

A group of translators have introduced us to an astonishing book of verse by Lev Ozerov, *Portraits Without Frames* (2018), fifty intimate accounts of meetings with major Soviet figures, including Shalamov, ranging from fellow poets Anna Akhmatova and Boris Pasternak to artists and composers including Vladimir Tatlin and Shostakovich. His poem about Shalamov gives a wonderful evocation of his understated style:

I don't ask about Kolyma,
And he doesn't mention it:
As if it hadn't happened.
As he eats the bread,
He holds one hand
Just below his chin.
Crumbs fall
Into his palm.
Shalamov eats them greedily,
With particular relish.

The Penguin Book of Russian Poetry, published in 2015, dramatically changed the shape of Russian poetry. As you read on, the landscape becomes stranger and more unfamiliar, especially as you come to the late twentieth century. Almost 150 pages of post-war poetry, nearly thirty poets, most of them unfamiliar to many English-speaking readers. New names. A new poetic world. Our sense of Russian literature has changed dramatically in recent years.

Then there are the mid-twentieth century writers from central Europe. Like Grossman's *Kolchugin's Youth*, Stefan Zweig's *The World of Yesterday* was translated into English in the 1940s, but in the last twenty years, biographies and short stories and novels in translation have poured out, especially thanks to Pushkin Press. There is even a cartoon version of his last days during the war. For the first time, British and American readers could see why Zweig in his heyday, between 1918 and 1934, when he left Austria for almost a decade in exile, was such a huge figure in interwar Europe. In his memoir, *The World of Yesterday*, Zweig wrote 'I was the most translated writer in the world' – '[m]y success grew slowly greater, until every time I published a book twenty thousand copies were sold in Germany in the first few days after it came out[...]'.

After years of neglect, Zweig was rediscovered at the turn of the century. Pushkin Press alone have translated almost twenty novels, books of essays and short stories in twenty years. Wes Anderson's film, *The Grand Budapest Hotel* (2013), with Ralph Fiennes, based on Zweig's writings, introduced him to a larger public.

Unlike Zweig, his friend, Joseph Roth, was hardly known in Britain or America after the war. It didn't help that he came from Galicia and spent much of his adult life on the move, between Vienna, Berlin and Paris. Kafka spent his life in Prague and until 1933 Thomas Mann lived in Germany. Mann was almost sixty when he went into exile. By then he had already written *Death in Venice*, *Buddenbrooks* and *The Magic Mountain*. His reputation was assured. It wasn't just a matter of where Roth lived, of course. Like Zweig, Hitler's rise meant that he couldn't be published in Germany or, after 1938, in Austria. Personal factors played a part also. He was difficult, irascible, declined into alcoholism before an early death at forty-four.

It was *The Radetzky March* that led to his rediscovery. Two translations published by Penguin in the 1980s and '90s helped Roth find a larger audience and translations of Roth's work have appeared at the rate of almost one a year since the 1990s. In addition to the fiction, there was a brilliantly edited book of Roth's Letters in 2012, essays and journalistic pieces, and a superb study by Dennis Marks, *Wandering Jew: The Search for Joseph Roth* (2011), which explored his roots in the small border-towns of Galicia. Above all, though, it was Michael Hofmann who championed Roth, translating and editing him, writing essays, attacking Stefan Zweig as inferior to Roth in a famous essay in *The London Review of Books* in 2010.

Thanks to the translator Len Rix and Pushkin Press, the Hungarian writer, Antal Szerb, burst upon the scene in the early 2000s, when he translated four novels in seven years. 'Szerb belongs with the master novelists of the twentieth century,' said *The Daily Telegraph*. The *Guardian* called him 'a master novelist'. Szerb was born in Hungary in 1901, the son of assimilated Jewish parents but he was baptised a Catholic. He travelled through Europe in the 1920s but returned to Hungary where he published his first novel, *The Pendragon Legend* (1934), a tale of mysticism and romance, set in a Welsh castle. Then came *Journey by Moonlight* (1937), the story of a young Hungarian businessman on his honeymoon in Italy. In 1944, Szerb was deported to a Nazi prison camp. He was executed during a forced march near the end of the war. Now, seventy-five years later, he has been rediscovered.

The discovery of Szerb was partly a matter of context. He was one of a group of major Hungarian writers who were translated into English after the fall of Soviet Communism. Sandor Marai was not published in English until the mid-1990s and then *Embers* (1942) was translated in 2000 and adapted for the stage by Christopher Hampton in 2006, starring Jeremy Irons and Patrick Malahide. Imre Kertesz was awarded the Nobel Prize in 2002 and *Fateless*, *Kaddish for an Unborn Child* and *Liquidation*, translated in the 1990s and early 2000s, were all republished soon after.

Like Roth, Bruno Schulz was born in Galicia in 1892, today part of Ukraine. His stories, *The Street of Crocodiles*, and his novel, *Sanatorium Under the Sign of the Hourglass*, were published in the 1930s, and were later translated and adapted as films and for the theatre. There are references to Schulz in the works of writers from Cynthia Ozick and Nicole Krauss and Jonathan Safran Foer.

David Vogel (1891–1944) was another itinerant writer. Born in the Russian Pale, he was unable to settle or lay down roots anywhere. He moved to Paris, briefly emigrated to Palestine, spent time in Poland and Berlin, and returned to Paris. After the German invasion, he escaped to south-east France, buried his manuscripts in a garden, was later caught by the Germans and deported to Auschwitz, where he was killed in 1944. Vogel has been championed by a handful of scholars, many of them in Israel, and by Scribe publishers in Australia who have translated two novels, *Viennese Romance* and *Married Life,* and *Two Novellas* (all published in 2013).

Mihail Sebastian was born Iosif Mendel Hechter in Romania 1907. He died on 29 May 1945, after being hit by a truck on his way to teach a class on Balzac. He was only thirty-eight. His journal was smuggled out of Romania by his brother Benu in the diplomatic pouch of the Israeli embassy in Bucharest when he emigrated from Romania to Israel in 1961. It was published in the US in 2000 and in the UK in 2003 as *Journal 1935–1944* and was hailed as a classic by Philip Roth and Arthur Miller among others. Since then four of his novels have been translated, including *For Two Thousand Years* (2016).

There are many people to thank for this literary revolution. Small new publishers including Pushkin Press, Scribe, Peter Owen and New York Review Books have led the way. Brilliant translators like Michael Hofmann, Anthea Bell, Len Rix, Boris Dralyuk and Robert and Elizabeth Chandler have introduced us to some of these great central European and Soviet writers. Critics have also played a huge role. John Gray has been writing about the Jewish Romanian writer, Mihail Sebastian, Shalamov and the Polish artist and writer, Jozef Czapski, in his book reviews for *The New Statesman*, Clive James wrote about Zweig in *Cultural Amnesia* and Nicholas Lezard, was one of the first critics to introduce British readers to Antal Szerb, in his much-missed Saturday column in *The Guardian*.

What explains this explosion? It was partly the rediscovery of central and east Europe and Soviet writers after the Fall of Communism in 1989/91. Roth's translator, Michael Hofmann, once said at Jewish Book Week that it was as if writers like Zweig and Roth had suddenly emerged from 'the deep freeze of history.'

For more than forty years countries like Hungary and Poland seemed on the margins of Europe, hard to get to, neglected and condescended to, lumped together as 'Eastern Europe'. Milan Kundera's famous essay, *The Tragedy of Central Europe* in *The New York Review of Books* (26 April 1984) changed all that. 'What does Europe mean to a Hungarian, a Czech, a Pole?' he asked. 'For a thousand years their nations have belonged to the part of Europe rooted in Roman Christianity. They have participated in every period in its history. For them, the word "Europe" does not represent a phenomenon of geography but a spiritual notion synonymous with the word "West".'

Over the next twenty years, European historians like Norman Davies (*Europe: A History*, 1996), Mark Mazower (*Dark Continent: Europe's 20th Century*, 1998), Tony Judt (*Postwar*, 2005) and Timothy Snyder (*Bloodlands*, 2010) shifted their gaze from London, Paris and Berlin to east and south-east Europe. It is no coincidence that they were all writing after the fall of Communism. In the opening paragraph of Tony Judt's history of post-war Europe, he writes, 'I first decided to write this book while

changing trains at the Westbahnhof, Vienna's main railway terminus. It was December 1989, a propitious moment. I had just returned from Prague, where the playwrights and historians of Vaclav Havel's *Civic Forum* were dislodging a Communist police state and tumbling forty years of 'real existing Socialism' into the dustbin of history... 'A political earthquake was shattering the frozen topography of post-World War II Europe.' Norman Davies wrote in the Introduction to his history of Europe, 'seventy years of totalitarian Soviet rule built huge mental as well as physical curtains across Europe. [...] When the chains of communism melted away, it enabled them to greet, in Vaclav Havel's phrase, "The Return to Europe".'

We may have neglected east European literature, but east European writers felt part of a larger European culture, which included London and Paris. On the morning of 2 September 1939, the Polish painter Jozef Czapski slipped a slim volume of André Gide's memoirs into his coat pocket and headed off to war with invading Nazi forces. Not long after, writes John Gray, in his review of Czapski's *Lost Time: Lectures on Proust in a Soviet Prison Camp,* Czapski lay in a Soviet camp hospital 'feverishly reciting lines from Baudelaire and whispering remembered passages from Proust'. In the same article Gray recalls how Shalamov devoured a copy of Proust in the Gulag. 'Proust,' Shalamov wrote, 'was more valuable than sleep.'

On 18 April 1944 Mihail Sebastian in Bucharest wrote in his journal, 'This morning's air-raid warning caught me at the *liceu* [...] The terrible silence of a deserted city [...] Yesterday I happened to open a volume of Baudelaire.' His journal is full of references to Jane Austen and Balzac, Byron, Gide and D.H. Lawrence.

On 1 August 1944, the day the Warsaw Uprising unexpectedly began, Czesław Miłosz lay face down in a field, with machine-gun bullets zipping over his head. He refused to let go of the book he was carrying, *The Collected Poems of T.S. Eliot* in the Faber & Faber edition. In his review in *The New York Review of Books* of Miłosz's *Collected Poems*, Al Alvarez described this as 'a typical day in the life of Central European Man'.

From Bucharest to Warsaw and the Gulag, for these writers, the classics of western Modernism were part of a shared heritage not something from another Europe.

After 1989, at the same time as historians were rediscovering central and east Europe, tourists started to visit cities like Prague, Cracow and Budapest. No longer behind the Iron Curtain, it became clear these cities were among the jewels of Europe. Publishers started to translate writers from mid-twentieth-century east Europe. Writers who had been ignored by the Communist regimes, killed in the Holocaust and forgotten in the west, received rave reviews in the literary press.

There was something else about these writers. They wrote brilliantly about Big History: Stalingrad and Soviet Communism, the end of what Zweig called 'The Age of Security' and the rise of Fascism and antisemitism in Europe. They brought to life the great dramas of twentieth-century European history.

It wasn't just Big History, it was Terrible History. In 1948, Karl Jaspers wrote that Germans 'came face to face with experiences in which we had no inclination to read Goethe, but took up Shakespeare, or the Bible, or Aeschylus, if it was possible to read at all'. What Jaspers meant was that in dark times we can only turn to certain writers. He was raising the bar when he spoke of Aeschylus and the Bible. But if you are trying to take stock of what happened in the Soviet Union in the mid third of the twentieth century, you might reasonably think that only writers like Grossman, Babel and Shalamov will do. Or if you wanted to know what it was like to live through Romanian antisemitism or the collapse of the Habsburg empire, then Sebastian or Joseph Roth wonderfully evoked the interwar years.

Perhaps that's why the centre of gravity of modern literature has shifted dramatically, from London, Paris and Berlin to Poland and Romania. Twenty-five years ago, this would have been inconceivable. Long-ignored cities like Czernowitz, Odessa and Lwów and regions like Galicia and Bukovina have been rediscovered.

Third, most of these writers were Jewish. Jewish culture came out of the margins of literary criticism. I mentioned Trilling. How often did he write about Jewish writers? Or F.R. Leavis and T.S. Eliot? It is no coincidence that so many of these rediscovered European writers were Jews. In large part, they were marginalised not just because they were from obscure parts of central and east Europe, but also because they were Jewish.

This was in part because Jewish critics found it hard to get jobs in English departments in Britain or in America before the 1950s and critics like Trilling, Hartman and Bloom thought it best to play safe and write about the English canon in their early years. Trilling's first two books were about E.M. Forster and Arnold, Hartman and Bloom started out by writing about the Romantic poets. Even George Steiner, who did so much to introduce writers and thinkers from central Europe to English-speaking readers, started out writing books about Tolstoy and Dostoevsky, tragedy and essays about French and German culture. Writing about Steiner in the *TLS* in 1995, Dan Gunn spoke of 'Steiner's intense and dramatic sense of his own Jewishness'. True, but only up to a point. The absences are fascinating. Steiner was not interested in any of the writers I have mentioned here or in the Yiddish-speaking culture of east Europe or the Russian Pale. Babel is the only one of these writers Trilling wrote about.

Comparative literature barely existed in the fifties. Outside modern languages departments who could read these writers in the original? English departments were where the action was. All this has changed. Jewish-European writers have suddenly received their due.

This revolution isn't just about fiction. Family memoirs like Edmund de Waal's *The Hare with Amber Eyes* (2010) and recent works of non-fiction like *East West Street* (2016) and *The Ratline* (2020) by Philippe Sands have introduced British readers to extraordinary stories about east Europe.

Crucially, a new generation of critics and scholars began to write about the Holocaust and Stalinism in a very different way. Not just about the workings of the totalitarian state but the scale of Nazi and Stalinist atrocities. Readers wanted to know more about what it was like to live in these societies and turned to the extraordinary accounts of writers like Grossman, Shalamov and Czesław Miłosz.

Often, these writers themselves had tragic personal stories – Bruno Schulz, shot by a Gestapo officer in 1942; Stefan Zweig and his wife committed suicide in Brazil, a few months earlier; Mihail Sebastian, who having survived years of antisemitism in Romania, was killed in an accident in May 1945, days after the war ended. Szerb was beaten to death in a concentration camp, Vogel was killed in Auschwitz, Babel was shot by a firing squad and his body was thrown into a communal grave.

Many of these writers were also refugees, moving from one place and language to another. Who knew where Joseph Roth was from or where he belonged? Belonging was the subject of one of his greatest stories, *The Emperor's Bust*. Roth lived out of suitcases all his life, as he moved from Galicia to Vienna, then to Berlin and Paris. 'He lives out of two suitcases,' wrote his translator Michael Hofmann, 'he is a Jew in Austria, an Austrian in Germany, and a German in France.' After Stefan Zweig left Austria, he was constantly on the move: London, New York, finally Brazil, until he committed suicide there during the war. David Vogel moved around Europe all his short life.

Exile had been a largely marginal subject during the mid-twentieth century and the focus was on extra-territorial writers like Beckett in Paris or Nabokov in America, but then in recent years, critics became interested in displacement and loss as some of the great subjects of modern literature. Roth and Zweig became interesting because they lived in exile not despite the fact they were refugees.

Jewishness, exile, coming from the margins of central Europe, had all contributed to the marginalisation of these writers. The world they came from seemed remote. Remember Neville Chamberlain's famous words about Czechoslovakia, 'a far-away country between people of whom we know nothing'? He could have been speaking of anywhere in central and east Europe. It wasn't just our attitudes to these writers that has changed. Our sense of Europe has been transformed. As a result, a whole generation of central and east European refugee writers have been rediscovered. The canon is shifting fast. It shows no sign of slowing.

It is not just about the canon, which writers we admire. It is also about the kind of modern literature we are drawn to: witness and testimony, realism, terrible atrocities and violence, the decline of societies, the rise of antisemitism and extremism. Works of literary modernism from London and Paris seem less appealing suddenly in these dark times since 9/11 and the financial crisis. Suddenly, writers from far away and long ago don't seem remote anymore. They speak to us with a new urgency.

Three Poems
SARAH WEDDERBURN

Apple orchard

Trees with gnarled branches, their bark scratchy.
If I stand in the light, am I blocking the light?
A question like a stain, ingrained.

At a time of stone blue and starch, when laundry was labour, Jane left the sheets
in a tin bath and went out to feed the hens. Looking for her unmarried sister, she said,
'Mary will put them through the mangle. She has nothing else to do.'

(Mary was busy. She was up an old apple tree, with a book.)

The sun shone. Mary was slow coming down the tree. Her white dress moved in and out
of shadow as she came through the orchard.

Jane, who listened to her husband, hissed, 'Women! What's to be done with them?'

Muslin once white, now yellow, like mutton fat.
If you render fat, are you giving it back?

The two Misses Clark ran the little school. They had us carry benches, which we called
forms, into the orchard.

There they arranged a tableau of *King Cophetua and the Beggar Maid*, with a group of senior
girls dressed and positioned to resemble the figures in the Burne-Jones painting.

For a long time the girls stood very still under the apple trees. We sat on the forms, with
pink blossom falling, and gazed at them, frozen in their poses.

Our future held its breath. Iris, who was the Beggar Maid, fainted.

Later, King Cophetua, whose name I forget, went away. She returned alone. Her
mother could not have her baby's linen flapping on the line, for all the village to see.

One meaning of render is 'cause to become'.
Love, mangled, is romance.
All romance has a coarse and brutal streak.

All the people on this earth could be others

Minuets and powdered hair. My ribbons pink and white. It was here beneath this
painted sky my first ever duke asked me to dance.

His coat was green brocade, with frogging, buttons of gold. He led me to a garden
filled with jasmine. Sky as blue and thick as velvet.

I was a girl, then, laughing on a swing. The stars flew up and down. I tossed my satin
slippers in the air like dice.

My paramour came visiting with gillyflowers. They splayed their scented petals
after he had left. Giddy with first love, I slipped towards a second, then a third.

Next spring, they hurried me away. You would soon be born. When summer came,
beneath the sumptuous roar of riverbank trees, we lay in milky meditation, you and I.

Two precious years we stayed. Your baby fingers pulled at daisies in wet grass. You
gazed at your muddied hands. Taught me life, better than Montaigne.

Time has passed. Now, I tend my arbour. Old admirers, kind with age, file back.
I deadhead roses while they tell adventures I forget, filling my dreams.

Too long, my dreams have shamed my drift from this princeling to that. Shamed
my blue eyes I thought more valuable than me.

All the people on this earth could be others. Look how my unborn babies wave down
from this gorgeous dome. So many different little noses!

They play safely in the clouds, my might-have-beens. Come, take tea with me,
my son. When must you leave again for Paris?

On not picking the cherries

This place. Or that *litmus* comes
from *lichen.* A singer's voice in
an early song. Words cutting ice
with Axel jumps. Skies out of context,

white-light mornings, breathing – those
will do it. It doesn't take much. I'll riff on
loss or doves or tennis balls, acid in slow-mo
replay. Or on basil, growing for us

like weed. Nightingales, potato harvesters,
pesto work as well, I find, as prods
to write, and – *zounds!* – *zoon*
being *son* in Dutch catapults me

into orbit, fast as catastrophe. Also
donkeys knitted for lifeboats. Facemasks
with faces on. Insane. But since we hurled
that bottle at our ship, I have tried to keep you

unwritten, while that tree – *cerezo, ciliegio,
Kirschbaum* – gets redder, riper, sweeter,
black with birds, and I do nothing.
Ask me. Come and get me.

Three Poems

ALI LEWIS

Art

Thunder clears its throat.
The cloud is almost black

and the shape of Scotland,
like its own weather map.

The rain dribbles shorthand
on the window, and obscures

the crotchets of the birds
on the stave of the fence,

who don't sing their notes,
but faithfully represent.

Giants

Now I'm the same height as I was then
as a toddler on my small father's shoulders

when I squeezed his ears with my doughnut
knees held on with my hands over his glasses

I feel a simultaneous kinship with the son
and the father and the ghost that is me

remembering the boy piloting an adult body
he could never hope to understand

the grown-up stumbling clumsy blindfold
trying to navigate the world with a child's eyes

and the man watching himself balance joy
with safety a burden he can feel but not see.

Like Words

When I was taught each drop
is flattened underneath by the air's resistance
to its falling, as if what looked like nothing

cared, I began to picture the rain,
wrongly, it transpires, as bullets in reverse,
retracing their paths to the muzzle,

but imagine if it did all come back to you
like that, and you got soaked. How much
you'd rejoice. How much it would hurt

Elegy for Alison
OLIVIA BYARD

Trionic Veloped

('Sweden's stylish new mobility aid')
i.m. Alison Byard

Your burble about this rushes
to be heard – its sporty look, light frame
detachable wheels you dreamt of
for your cycling marathons –
     and now out of breath,
you wheeze, chemo-bald again but delighted
to explain – you can clamp
on the light-touch brakes and rest a while
on its seat.
    I admit I was
doubtful – its price, and also,
the princess-gold pumps you chose
as sole footwear for a wet week
in Snowdonia.
    But your vigorous paean
propels me away from your latest funeral plan,
and back to a Friday night in our old flat –
you in a tinfoil helmet, humming Van Morrison
as henna cooks into your hair and
precision-painting toenails in cotton-wool
cocoons – me waiting, as usual,
deep in my latest book.
   Until your nails dry at last,
we head down to the Cape of Good Hope,
to its swirls of lit shadows –
and hurl our freed selves again,
into the surging, roiling, crowd.

Taking Funeral Notes

It is when you decide on
Lebanese cuisine, that I quake.

'Ash Wednesday' is easy to find –
those Eliot lines you love. The church,
ditto. Blue and white flowers – I note
that down – lilies, query irises? Cornflowers?!

But Lebanese cuisine – how do
we do that? When you quip
you'd make it yourself (only of course
you won't be there), I nearly ask you
to store it in your big freezer until
it's needed.

Instead I say, 'You're being so brave',
and curse my words throughout
the curt silence that follows.

What I meant though, what I wish
I'd said – is that we all have choices,
and I was noting yours down – to put two fingers
up to death, dictate its first steps, nail
the bastard down to your wishes
before the offing. Instead, I scrawl,
Lebanese food, somehow!

Night Song

(For Ali)

Where the crammed gulch
spills russets over tilting fields –
sudden trills,
   as tiny birds burst into song
from hedgerows and meadow.
    Through the cool
refining breeze, high sounds race down
through dimming channels.
    I wander, stop, wonder –
stand still each few footsteps.
Until song swells to chorus,
and I'm gratefully subsumed.

The Enthralling Alfred Kazin
TONY ROBERTS

'It is a horrible book, and the more dangerous, because it sounds (or will sound to so many people) plausible,' Cleanth Brooks complained to Allen Tate in January 1943. Alfred Kazin's *On Native Grounds* had been published the year before. Brooks, an exponent of the New Criticism, was complaining of the negative comments on 'The Formalists' in the book. He was correct. *On Native Grounds*, which launched Kazin's career-long study of American literature, is a highly plausible book. More than plausible, it is comprehensive, profound and partisan, a self-confessed attempt at moral history, the summation of a lifetime's reading by a young man of twenty-seven who had barely begun.

It was an astonishing debut, really a series of mini-intellectual biographies relating to the emergent 'struggle for realism' in fiction and criticism from 1890 to 1940. Although Kazin wrote essay after essay with insight and passion for another sixty years, collecting them in such books as the substantial *Contemporaries* (1963), he could never better it. No wonder it made his name as America's go-to 'literary radical'. It was to be more than forty years before he tried something remotely similar, in *An American Procession* (1984), though time had cooled the radical passion to ingratiating warmth.

Kazin's motivation lay in his sense of literary criticism as an exalted calling. He committed himself fully to it, being 'first astonished by gifts that I do not possess, then excited by the chance to make contact with them through my analysis'. Elsewhere in his self-lacerating *Journals* (2011) he recorded that, 'As a critic, I read and read certain texts, the beloved ones, so as to *possess* them.' The proximity to greatness and the possession of books luminous to the point of sacredness, led him to adopt his subjects: 'the writers as characters in my book were friends and the most encouraging people in the world to write about,' he acknowledged in a 1995 preface to *On Native Grounds*.

The impulse was always toward intellectual biography and narrative. 'I was confident that I could read the mind behind a book,' Kazin wrote in *New York Jew*. Over a long writing life he pursued – with 'perception to the pitch of passion' in Henry James's phrase – what Melville called in an 1851 letter to Hawthorne 'the inmost leaf', the writer perfectly unfolded within himself. (Kazin borrowed the image for a book title.) He wrote privately of his mission as the drive to define the 'individual core of talent, "the gift"'. His 'joy' in so doing was in line with Emerson's perception that criticism and commentary, 'if they are not in the service of enthusiasm and ecstasy, are idle at best'.

Kazin's dedication to American literary history, as subject, paralleled his need for it as myth in his life. He was born in Brownsville, Brooklyn, in 1915 to Jewish immigrant parents. The difficulties of his early life led to his romanticising an America from which he always felt something of an outsider:

The past, the past was great: anything American, old, glazed, touched with dusk at the end of the nineteenth century, still smouldering with the fires lit by the industrial revolution, immediately set my mind dancing. (*A Walker in the City*)

He was, as he declared, 'seeking *sanctions*', finding them in the example of those American writers who lived artistically as well as personally isolated. The fact that Emmerson, Thoreau, Whitman and Melville had lived encouraged him. Like them, perhaps, he was a writer 'looking for a place to put his mind'.

Kazin attended City College, became a needy, pushy reviewer in 1934, and then earned an M.A. from Columbia in 1938, the year he married the first of four wives. His biographer Richard M. Cook noted evidence in the early reviews of a 'penchant for responding to writers as historical actors and personalities whose moral qualities he closely associates with their literary achievement'. His heroes were the independents, Van Wyck Brooks and especially Edmund Wilson ('the conscience of two intellectual generations'). While the life of the mind became Kazin's obsession, he charted the growth of his own in three atmospheric autobiographies: *A Walker in the City* (1951), *Starting Out in the Thirties* (1965) and *New York Jew* (1978). In the second he described his life as that of a Jewish New York intellectual who avoided the solemnity of the Marxism of his peers: 'I felt myself to be a radical, not an ideologue; I was proud of the revolutionary yet wholly literary tradition in American writing to which I knew that I belonged.'

And so he wrote *On Native Grounds* to describe 'the rise of the modern in American literature, its sensibility, its liveliness, its protest'. He focused on the realist tradition, feeling himself appealing to 'the spirit of the age'. Vernon Parrington's *Main Currents in American Thought* (1927) had been greatly influential in crystallising the modern liberal tradition. It was to provide Kazin, as Cook explained, 'with a means of selection and a dramatic structure'.

On Native Ground is in three parts, following the ebb and flow of progressivism. This is narrative literary history, concerned always with the movement of the mind, rather than the detailed examination of individual works. 'The Search for Reality' (1890–1917) deals with the emergence of realism, with William Dean Howells, Edith Wharton, Theodore Dreiser, Stephen Crane, Frank Norris and others. The second part, 'The Great Liberation' (1918–1929), offers a more conflicted view where the admired likes of Ellen Glasgow and Willa Cather meet the forces of cynicism (H.L. Mencken) and reaction (Paul Elmer More, Irving Babbitt and other New Humanists).

Kazin wanted to study 'our alienation *on* native grounds – the interwoven story of our need to take up our life on our own grounds, and the irony of our possession.'

Progressivism in the shape of Hemingway, Fitzgerald and Dos Passos sailed too close to nihilism. Though he believed a certain disengagement to be vital, the writer's task was to improve America, not dismiss it.

'The Literature of Crises' (1930–1940) describes a literature of social realism – the novels of Erskine Caldwell, James T. Farrell and John Steinbeck – which Kazin finds both committed and wanting. His greatest antagonism is reserved for the literary critics, the Marxists and the reactionary Formalists, who have marginalised the older liberal tradition. Finally, looking for the optimistic spirit at a time of international turbulence, Kazin turns to the wider, more palatable 'literature of social description' in New Deal America, which includes the Works Progress Administration (WPA), photography, biography and history.

Like a Dickens novel, Kazin's dashingly confident history teems with characters caught with an image or a touch of colour: 'Hamlin Garland acted as the bandmaster of realism'; 'It was if [Sherwood Anderson] had been brought up in a backwater, grown quaint and self-willed, a little "queer," a drowsing village mystic, amidst stagnant scenes.' Of Crane, he writes, 'He baited the universe but never those village citizens who are as benign in his work as small-town fathers in the *Saturday Evening Post.*' There are many insightful one-liners: 'the symbols Hemingway employed to convey his sense of the world's futility and horror were always more significant than the characters who personified them.' Of Faulkner's characters we learn: 'though the energy that drives them along is torrential, we do not see *them* intensely; we see everything under *conditions* of intensity.'

Kazin joys in extravagant rhetorical flourishes, as in his treatment of the lost generation: 'They had a special charm – the Byronic charm, the charm of the specially damned; they had seized the contemporary moment and made it their own; and as they stood among the ruins, calling the ruins the world, they seemed so authoritative in their dispossession, seemed to bring so much craft to its elucidation, that it was easy to believe that all the roads really had led up to them'. The imagery is always atmospheric: 'Soon enough, the masters of aestheticism and the prophets of languor rose from the ashes of the fin de siècle'; 'No longer did the American realist have to storm the heavens, or in the grimness of creation build his books with massive blocks of stone.'

If one stopped to quibble about Kazin's judgements one might have questions. Kazin himself admitted to having over-cherished Howells. When he writes of the 'immense distinction' of Carl Sandburg's Lincoln biography, we are more likely to remember Edmund Wilson's quip , 'The cruellest thing that has happened to Lincoln since being shot by Booth was to have fallen into the hands of Carl Sandburg.' Does Crane resemble so much in spirit Fitzgerald? Does Eliot's critical style bear 'the overtones of an inexhaustible disillusion', or is it rather the poetry? Is Farrell 'Proustian?'

And what of Marxism and the New Criticism which Cleanth Brooks so worried about? Kazin knew something about Marxist ideologues, having matured among the anti-Stalinist left of 'Partisan Review'. Marxism he declares has 'something almost too prehensile about it

– it lends itself to too many different uses'. His dislike of the 'Formalists' of New Criticism, however, stems from his simplification of it as a method of divorcing book and author.

Kazin was not a critic of poetry and so creates something of a straw man here. Beneath its surface protest against critical sloppiness, he sees a sinister, loose grouping of academic reactionaries who look for scientifically grounded criticism and prize the exclusiveness of modern poetry. This 'group' – Southern-led and therefore a useful counterpoint to Northern (New York) Marxists – also deplores Northern materialism and egalitarianism. Despite Brooks's fears and Kazin's continuing enmity – he later compared it to the hobby of tinkering with a car – the New Criticism as a method of textual analysis would dominate teaching for many years.

On Native Grounds, as Kazin noted in his 1995 preface (with a dig at recent trends), 'was written out of an old-fashioned belief that literature conveys central truths about life, that it is indispensable to our expression of the human condition and our struggle for a better life.' Most of his reviewers must have agreed. Irwin Edman, Columbia philosophy professor, wrote a front-page review for the *New York Herald Tribune* (Books), calling its publication 'not only a literary but a moral event.' Orville Prescott in *The New York Times* judged Kazin would 'take his place in the first rank of American practitioners of the higher literary criticism.' He wondered too how Kazin had managed the time to eat and sleep while digesting whole libraries.

Forty years later the 'wunderkind' did not have the same vitality, or at least the same perspective. In 1982 he complained, 'Before I came to the end of my book in 1942 the moral bankruptcy of many left-wing writers left me, though still radical, less convinced of the "necessary" connection between literature and social criticism.' 'The Function of Criticism today', in the wide-ranging *Contemporaries*, ends with the thought 'We must practice criticism on the older writers lest they harden into the only acceptable writers. We must learn to practice criticism on the newer writers, to bind them more truly to our own experience.' In *An America Procession: The Major American Writers from 1830 to 1930 – The Crucial Century* (1984). Kazin turns to the older.

With *An American Procession* we are in the hands of an ageing, eminent critic no less confident in his assertions but we sense less speculatively so. The key difference between this book and the first is that now Kazin narrows his focus to twenty favourites. Consequently the tone is more generally admiring and empathetic (except in regard to Pound and perhaps the un-American James). Otherwise it is quintessential Kazin. He begins with the founding of a national American literature when the 'God-intoxicated' Emerson left the church, ending with the triumph of modernism in the 1920s and the recognition of those modernists *avant la lettre* Henry Adams, Melville, Whitman and Dickinson.

According to his biographer, *An American Procession* (1984) is flawed by a number of things: its failure to take the temper of the times in which it was written; it's inability to find a literary-historical structure; its self-indulgence in ignoring other critics; and its narrative of decline. Admittedly Kazin does trace a darkening promise. Yet one perceived weakness is to me its strength. In keeping his subjects – shaped as always into characters – to himself, Kazin offers a series of lively monologues that in their atmospheric intimacy give the effect of conversation.

In his preface the unnamed Harold Bloom takes criticism, in a reference to a 'debased Freudianism' used to 'exaggerate the natural rivalry' of canonical writers, some of whom were actually friends while others isolates. 'Isolated' is a leitmotif as central to the book as 'insurgency' was to the more radical *On Native Grounds*. Kazin's nineteenth-century heroes endured their isolation, both the cause and cost of their art. He cites Emerson's late recognition 'that the infinite universe cannot be domesticated to man's religious needs. This became the lonely stoic note of America's problem writing in Melville, Dickinson, Mark Twain, Stephen Crane, Wallace Stevens.' A journal entry from January 1957 elaborates:

> such loneliness is an act of criticism, and like all real criticism suffers from an essential formlessness; tends to express itself in fits and starts, in marginal glosses. Hence the lumber of Hawthorne's stories and Emerson's journals and Poe's tales: the profound inner formlessness of Whitman.

As Howells led earlier, so the historian Henry Adams launches *An American Procession*. Kazin's is a bold portrait of a man who viewed 'History's mad acceleration into "chaos"', an appropriate choice since Adams was the scion of American presidents *and* a harbinger of modernism: 'Henry Adams, who despised the masses, despaired of progress, declared himself a failure, and drew the last drop of bitterness from his experience, has turned out to be one of the ruling myth makers of American history.'

The book shows rare skill in keeping personalities and the movement of their thoughts before the reader's eye. Kazin's method is to surround his subject, darting in with an aphorism here, a subtle metaphor there, a poetic touch, a parallel, a grand statement such as this which springs from his excellent treatment of Melville: 'If ever there was a style that belonged to America's own age of discovery, a style innocently imperialist, romantic, visionary, drunk on symbols, full of the American brag, this is it.' His empathy never over-relies on biographical props or dallies on books for character and thematic analyses.

Kazin loves counterpointing as a linking device. So Adams and Eliot are the sceptics of the prologue. Henry James would have found Dickinson's poems embarrassing since 'She was not in the "real" world, society'. Nature is other to Emerson yet other self to Thoreau; Faulkner shares Hawthorne's obsession with a locale but is really more like the rhetorically embattled Melville. Crane is teamed with Hemingway ('Style was primary with him, as it was to be with the Hemingway he often anticipates') while Theodore Dreiser, like Whitman, 'disturbed the secularized Protestant elect who had replaced religion with morality and morality with

propriety'. And Adams, Twain and Dreiser felt 'mechanistic theories' of the *fin de siècle* sanctioned their disenchantment.

Kazin's perceptions are, as always, stylishly expressed and often biographical in nature: 'Emerson owed much of his influence to his private aura; he impressed by seeming inaccessible'; 'The artist in Dreiser was always stronger than the man'; 'At every stage of his life [Hemingway] found himself a frontier appropriate to his fresh needs as a sportsman and his ceremonial needs as a writer.' Then there is the novelistic flair:

> Emerson was an organic writer and instinctive stylist who even on the platform seemed to be waiting for his own voice to astonish him. Dickinson's lifetime investment in the poem as miniature made her see that only the barest lyric could render so much finality, the purest personal fantasy of travelling into death with the mind radiantly poised for novelty.

The book sparks with literary insights: 'Eliot in America could never have written with such lordliness'; in Hawthorne's unfinishable novels: 'the characters, having this awful symbolic weight to bear, kept turning into each other and getting lost'; 'It is the force of the repressed that Poe made his drawing card'; 'Whitman's time sense is one of suspension. There is a longing somehow not to be fulfilled'; Dickinson 'unsettles, most obviously, by not been easily locatable'; 'There was nothing in James's world to conspire about but the secret love to which money is attached'; 'Crane's "lines," as he called his poems, are just that; they breathe an air of satisfaction, they seem too easily satisfied with their contemptuous brevity'; 'Dos Passos sometimes resembles one of those early movie directors resurrected for his "technique" at the Museum of Modern Art'; and Pound, whom Kazin would never forgive for his ardent antisemitism: 'was an assimilationist of genius, a ventriloquist able to reproduce alien and ancient voices, cadences, styles – often in wilful ignorance of the actual substance.'

Again we may wonder how original or astute specific judgments are and yet we are swept along in the general passion, as were a number of critics. 'With *An American Procession*, Alfred Kazin confirms a reservation in the front tier of the reviewing stand, next to his eminent predecessors Van Wyck Brooks and Edmund Wilson' – *The New York Times Book Review*; 'A sense of caring intimacy lifts Kazin's survey above the usual inventory of masterworks' – *The New Yorker*; 'The *Procession* is wonderfully exciting to read' – *The New Republic*.

Other reviewers apparently did not share the enthusiasm and the book was politely ignored. One reason his biographer cites is that it did not offer anything new to the critical debate, which is not surprising given Kazin's outsider hostility to an academia with which he was only fitfully engaged (A writer 'can be so exasperated by the intellectual togetherness of critical opinion' he announced in a 1960 review). Another is that these chapters are largely reworkings of earlier published pieces. Sometimes the joins show. His Poe is mostly a study of one book, for example, and we are told twice about

Adams 'scientific' approach and Eliot's confession that *The Waste Land* was 'just a piece of rhythmical grumbling'. Such criticism hardly mars the book.

Granted Kazin was of his time and even by 1984 that time was passing as the critical circus moved on to text and meaning. Yet the romantic in us can admire his commitment to the idea that criticism should show 'almost physical empathy'. His did. What he gave the reader – and can still give – is the bracing evidence of this. That is what enthrals.

Envoi to the Self
MICHAEL HELLER

'Envoi to the Self' is part of my 'Tibet Sequence', a series of poems loosely based on the French poet Victor Segalen's *Odes suivies de Thibet*. In his short life (1878–1919), Segalen, a medical doctor for the French navy, travelled extensively in Polynesia and the Far East. Like Gauguin, with whom he is often linked, Segalen was one of the great explorers of indwelling, of otherness. In his little-known 'Essay on Exoticism', he explores 'the notion of difference, the perception of Diversity, the knowledge that something is other than one's self. Exoticism's power is nothing other than the ability to conceive otherwise.' In *Odes suivies de Thibet*, he takes up his interests in Buddhist and Taoist thought, attempting at times to mimic the language of the Sages whose genius, compassion and knowledge of the illusory self he venerated. The critic Haun Saussy has written that Segalen's poems seem to be 'translated from a work that does not anywhere else exist'. My own poems, written in the spirit of Segalen's phrase 'to conceive otherwise' follow his habits of mimicry, seeking an opportunistic, even perhaps exploitive mingling of Segalen's thought and language with my own. Playing with his words and with mine, I have called these poems 'transpositions' and not 'translations', attempting in my own way to produce a language that does not elsewhere exist, possibly the goal of all poetry itself. All along, my aim has been to conjure an imagined, a timeless 'Tibet', a place not only of great and rugged beauty but of spiritual instruction and ethical hope.

I

Where the site, the ground,
    the middle between the self and the country promised to all?
The traveler travels. The seer holds it under his eyes.
    My own impoverished being no longer dominates.
Let the legendary names determine powers:
    Nepemako in Poyoul and Padma Skod,
Knas-Padma-Bskor.
    Let these coarse syllables aggregate the teachers.
Tell me again, wandering monk, furious seeker –
    where has a floodtide of wisdom emerged?
I have too many times doubted the contours of the world,
    denied the overwhelmed heart.
Like the implacable ever-circling Garuda, I find no place
    to land, no place to set body
and self in some commanding pose.
    Where is the background?
The undrawn curtain of the self's apotheosis?
    Where does my unabated desire live?
At what reception do you foresee it – at what point do you recognize it?
    O yon god still to be born and enthroned?
Is it in yourself or more than you, Pole-Tibet, First Emperor,
    or does hell truly burn, promising to be,
in lieu of glory and knowledge, the place to love and to understand?
    Let me be accomplished.

Useless, useless. I am there alone,
      and you are the face of the spectacle I self-created.
This fixated place transformed by appearance,
      given such assured density and depth.
I am entangled in you in this way, call it sacred or profane,
      O my failed country.
      At the height of this simulation, my whiteness
has been exposed, naked in the pupil of its own haggard eye.
      But I too bring my tricks, my bag of simulacra.
I split in two the moon that rises after so many suns,
      so many days and auroras.

Your moon and mine, dream moons because Time flaunts Space,
      hence the mockery. Deceptive being, mind and body,
I am speaking of the way you are addressed.
      Yes, I made more leaps and songs of love to you,
and they died in metaphors.
      May the time be. May this be the surrender.
A fall from haughtiness into joy,
      bringing forth a cry that bursts from the depths.
A fierce trembling like the caress from a volcano.
      No matter that the names played savagely with me,
as though twisting into my own viscera!
      Here is this high moment. I hold it for good,
for love itself to make me cry with pleasure.

Two Poems

MADELEINE PULMAN-JONES

Embassies

In Moscow, I lived opposite a row of embassies.
They rolled down the street like a sentence

off a polyglot's tongue.
One morning, I found a full stop

in front of the Estonian embassy:
a lump on my neck. It felt final,

and I knew denial was hopeless –
that the year had run out of breath.

Even in the day's new light,
the facades coloured a sunset –

The Netherlands was yellow, Japan was pink,
Estonia was the grey that comes before night.

I used to think that seeing was puzzling out –
that it was a kind of translation. For example,

I knew that if you looked hard enough,
you could find 'stone' in 'Estonia'.

But I never thought that I would see that far
into my own body, beyond the bare bones.

The scans that came after were anagrams
with no answers: PET-CT, x-ray.

They told me the answers were in the 'imaging',
in the orange glow that clung to my bones

the way a sunset clings to the horizon.

I catch death in birth's lining

I wear birth like a coat I have learned to take on and off
without a mirror. I catch death in birth's lining
as I turn out its sleeves.

My mother watches me tug at the cuffs, listens to
jokes to offset the mood, leans forward as I lay it down
on the back of her chair.

Now I turn out my arms to the sky, to the nurse who looks
for veins she can't see in the thickness of my skin.
But I'm thin-skinned,

no blood, only tears as she pins me
like a tailor making alterations – not there, not quite,
no flow.

Four times she forces the needle in and pushes,
sewing saltwater into the wound, stinging my skin.
Are you in pain?

It's in the vein. Please confirm your full name and date of birth.
My palms sweat and I'm afraid of forgetting myself,
over and over,

every day until they tell me it's dissolved, the cancer, and after,
until the words dissolve, the facts, infertility,
the risk of dying...

If dying is more than turning birth inside out, then how
does anyone do it? My arms are too weak even for pulling,
for putting off –

my mother leans back on my coat reading Blue Nights,
laughs occasionally, happy to tell me that Joan Didion
was smaller than she is.

And I'm smaller and smaller sitting here like the edge
of the evening when it all turns blue – my wrist
is getting dark, is it night,

is it nicer of me to stop myself from seeping out?
My neck bulges with the biggest thing I've ever borne –
it isn't even a baby.

Two Poems

PAUL MILLS

Supernatural

as when a loved child walks unhurt from a burning forest
into your open arms yet it's not her
or a long growl lichen-haired
mixes its breathing with the familiar

or your thoughts are interrupted suddenly
by the disturbed voice of a dead mother
by a surge in the air of a lost brother
sometimes they come back   see through your eyes

look look   they say   at some lovely thing
a green fir cone   a jumping fish   they see it
or when I'm playing a flute   one they made
so we hear their singing clustering with us

or the voice of a caribou skin
as I cut and loosen it from the body
saying *like this like this   do it like this
look how I give you myself still warm*

but sometimes not   sometimes fire won't talk
sparks into nothing   into wind that howls just to itself
sometimes I know only my own hands
that the only skill in them is mine

I hear roaring out of the dead steppe
on and on and on   to the air the stars
to where rock is rock   flayed by ice
and so raise my cry to the ancestors   *come*

tell us how to survive the dark
so we can crouch together by a fire
no strangeness in their flickering faces
feeling in its heat the desired lost

Nomads

you following herds followed by wolves
to where the sun a red flare

holds open a space between cloud and tundra
your own fires making extinct tracks

into boreal forest
not knowing you've crossed a quarter of the globe

out from behind the curve of it   slanting west

roads and towns of the Swabian Alb invisible
in the future

following new-melted tons of Lone and Danube

wing-beat and honk of night-flying geese
croak of ravens   eagle talons sliding out of the air

a long-thriving hunger swallowing you
some child-voice in you with its cry

bringing the wounded man   the lame woman

cold still weakening your grip   startling you
into exhausted numbness   driving you

closer towards each other's furious resolve
that no life possible must be lost

Two Poems
ALEXEY SHELVAKH
TRANSLATED BY J. KATES

An Epigram

Once I was a lilac, waiting
for water as if it were freedom.
I suffocated in the Universe
of a locked Heavenly Vault.

Song of the Composer of an Epic Poem

'Under the birch trees
the ants danced their automatic dances
and the maiden ants
bowed their inky-wax heads.

Under the birch trees
the wild strawberry blossomed,
while insects rode in their cutaneous coaches
on complaining springs.

Under the birch trees
a bullet breaks my body in half –
I drop down dead!
And my brethren in their ashen coats drop in chorus
each one crying out alone
under the birch trees!'

And a squirrel's shadow fell across the forehead
of the composer of the epic poem.

Grosseteste Part 2
'A solid and often brilliant magazine'
IAN BRINTON

The first issue of *Grosseteste Review* appeared in the spring of 1968 and the last volume, number fifteen, was published in 1984. As I mentioned in my earlier article on the Grosseteste Press, the initial aim had been to publish three issues of the new magazine each year, but this remarkable publication was to undergo some significant changes over the sixteen years of its existence. It was also to lend its name to Grosseteste Review Books which began in 1972 with John Hall's diary of poems titled *Days*. When the magazine's founding editor, Tim Longville, produced his *Grosseteste Descriptive Catalogue* in 1975 he devoted the last few pages to the *Review* itself and quoted some significant comments upon the way the whole venture had been received, ranging from John Freeman's assertion in *Cambridge Quarterly* that it was 'Widely regarded as the best of the little magazines' to Peter Finch's celebration in *Second Aeon*: 'And amidst all the shouting Grosseteste goes quietly on, a solid and often brilliant magazine.'

The first issue had been printed on the Stonefield Avenue Grosseteste Press and consisted of forty-eight pages, of which thirteen were prose. Gordon Jackson gave a very clear account of the early stages of the magazine when he wrote that it was all 'in handset type' but that it was here that the first problems started:

> The only way to make it easier was to get the prose set outside and do the poetry etc by hand, which we eventually did by the time we got to the Winter issue. From then on I was often journeying to Birstall in the West Riding to order new settings and return the used type. The *Review* could proceed, but the costs would rise.

These costs, along with the death in 1978 of John Riley, poet and business manager, led to the ending of what had become a major contribution to the world of British poetry in the second half of the twentieth century.

An awareness of the importance of what had been happening in America since the mid-sixties was made immediately evident in the magazine's first issue. Andrew Crozier had brought Carl Rakosi (Callman Rawley) back into the public eye after some thirty years of quiet since the days of the *Objective Anthology* and the new *Grosseteste Review* presented three appreciations of *Amulet*, the American poet's first publication after the breaking of his long silence. Bearing this in mind it seems appropriate that Crozier's own magazine *Wivenhoe Park Review* that he had started at Essex in 1965 should be advertised at the front of this new magazine under its new title *The Park*. The three reviews of *Amulet* were by John Hall, Barry MacSweeney and Tim Longville and, as the editor of this new magazine was to make very clear, from now on the Anglo-American association was here to stay.

Referring to Rakosi he complimented the American Objectivist's craft as a poet: 'A craft which owns and revels in its debt to Zukofsky and to Stevens, preserving and upon occasion decorating impression and object with fidelity, tact, rhythmic life.'

Rakosi's own recent poetry was also featured in the second issue of the magazine where it appeared alongside work by Lew Welch and Gilbert Sorrentino and the third issue of the year contained a substantial piece of prose by Joanne Kyger, the former wife of Gary Snyder. Kyger's 'Places to Go' was the first extract from what was to become the 1970 Black Sparrow Press edition published under the same title and in one of those little literary mysteries which can often be rather amusing it was one of Kyger's poems, 'The Hunt in the Wood: Paolo Uccello', that, later on, was mistakenly assumed to have been written by John Riley, making its appearance in the 1980 Grosseteste *Collected Poems*, a volume of major distinction which Gordon Jackson was to describe as both 'elegant and magnificent.'

According to Jackson 1969 was largely taken up with the second volume of the *Review* and there were again three issues running to fifty-six, forty-eight and sixty-four pages respectively. In 1970 volume three of the magazine became the last three issues to appear from the Grosseteste Press itself and as Jackson put it, 'In the endless battle between costs, time and labour we had arrived at an arrangement where the printing was done outside, and the print produced by Tim on an IBM typewriter, with underlining replacing italics.'

This third volume also had a complementary supplement which was advertised as a 'Special Catullus / Zukofsky Issue' containing an important essay by Cid Corman on 'Poetry as Translation'. Perhaps the ongoing lack of interest in what had been happening in American poetics could not have been made clearer by Corman, the editor of *Origin*:

> In the year's time or less since Celia and Louis Zukofsky's versions of Catullus have been available between covers, the book has been formidably attacked in *all* the respectable English periodicals (*The Times Literary Supplement* and *Encounter* most notably) and where it has been found acceptable has been quickly glossed over.

Corman's concern for the way in which reviewers were working is uncompromisingly clear:

> I feel no need to mince words in this matter. My relation as a frequent publisher of the Zukofskys and of many of these poems as they first occurred is too well-known. But my response to poetry is to poetry. A

reviewer scans what comes his way and in the short time given him attempts to judge what is, of necessity, beyond judgement. It would take as much imaginative effort to realize fully what is here – in these versions of Catullus – as went into the making of this book. And I have seen NO evidence as yet that anyone is willing to put in even a fraction of that effort. But judgement is readily passed. And the readers, the few there are, of open-mind and ready ear, are prevented from even approaching this 'possibility'.

Grosseteste Review was perhaps aimed at the open-minded reader who possessed a ready ear.

In March 1971 John Riley wrote a brief note to Michael Grant to say that 'Tim and I have now taken over the Grosseteste Review completely' and that whilst the editorial work was in the hands of Longville, Riley became 'lumbered with the finances'. These relative positions in terms of what was now called Grosseteste Review Press along with its subsidiary publications GR/EW Books can be seen in the opening statement of Longville's *Descriptive Catalague*:

Editorial (submissions of manuscripts or anything at all to do with work being or intended to be published:
  Tim Longville, 10 Consort Crescent, Commonside, Pensnett, Brierley Hill,
    Staffordshire, England.
Business (orders, enquiries, anything at all to do with the finances of the Press or of the Review):
  John Riley, 4 Gledhow Wood Close, Leeds 8, Yorkshire, England.

In his invaluable little account of both the Grosseteste and the Asgill Lincoln Presses, Gordon Jackson makes clear his own position in relation to the new avenue being opened:

Looking at my old copies it seems the last contribution I made to what now would become Grosseteste Review publications or Gr/ew Books was the cover for *The Lew Poems* in 1971. I also did the headings and cover lettering for Tim's splendid memorial volume for John Riley after his murder in 1978. So we [Gordon and Hélène] bowed out, and the continued success of the enterprise was all down to Tim. What energy! What perseverance! And the books kept coming. Sixteen of them are listed in the 'Descriptive Catalogue' as forthcoming. They would have run to four years' work in our old letterpress days, but with typewriter and commercial printer it was just a matter of money.

In 1973 a bumper volume of the magazine appeared containing four issues bound together in its 256 pages. The shift from separately published individual issues had come about as a result of cuts in Arts Council funding. Riley wrote to Michael Grant to tell him that as a result of the Midlands Arts Council not awarding them a grant that year Tim Longville was prepared to type the pages so that the work which was to include a wide range of contributors ranging from Hugh Kenner to Jeremy Prynne and George Oppen to Donald Davie could appear

as this one substantial publication:

We're going to produce this issue come what may... [and it] does show the Review at last really working; for my money it has at last got together people who have the talent to produce a literature, and who need this focus... One's personal shame at the state of literature in this country can be fruitful when one can do something about it, but given no outlet, it would be a bigger killer disease than boredom.

The new Grosseteste Review book publications (gr/ew books) started in 1972 with the appearance of John Hall's *Days* which was quickly followed by Denis Goacher's *Logbook* and Jack Collom's *blue heron & ibc*. The newness of this world of poetry had been registered by Basil Bunting in his comments upon Goacher's poems as requiring 'an attention the public has not yet given it'. Indeed the importance of the work being presented by this new press was also registered in Bunting's awareness that any lack of attention was 'perhaps because it is often remote from current fashions'; 'He has a voice of his own and it should be heard.'

The books kept appearing and in 1973 number nine in the series was Peter Riley's *The Linear Journal* about which Andrew Crozier was to comment in *The Spectator*: '... [He is] engaged in an attempt to write poetry that can be totally inclusive of a man's serious interests... [He is] part of the real direction of English poetry now. I don't suppose, though, that very many will notice for some time yet.' It was quickly followed by number ten, John Riley's *Ways of Approaching*, a collection that included the first three sections of 'Czargrad', a poem the appearance of which had prompted Jeremy Prynne to write to Tim Longville: 'I can't help thinking of some sweet rain falling steadily over the fields, gracefully immune to human denial; and JR moved even more than moving others, the elegist turning to psalms.'

The first three issues of volume seven of the magazine appeared in one volume in 1974 and Iain Sinclair rubbed shoulders with Roy Fisher, John Wilkinson with both William Bronk and Joel Oppenheimer. The volume was also accompanied by a letter pointing out the direction for the future:

The Review for 1975 will consist of a series of pamphlets. With one exception each of these will be devoted to a single author. The total number of pages in these pamphlets will be roughly equal to the number of pages in a normal year's issues.
  In 1976 we hope to find financial and technical ways to return to more frequent and more orthodox magazine issues, as well as to continue publishing pamphlets and books.

This way of supplementing issues of the magazine began with the fourth number of volume seven being James Koller's *Shannon, Who Was Lost Before*. The Illinois poet and novelist who had edited *Coyote's Journal* had had to wait some time before this appearance of his 'road novel' and Longville put down 'for the record' that 'it took six or more years for the desire to do this book to come together with the necessary finance'. As he stoically went on to say: '... in the little press world it often does take that long or longer'. That short novel's final appearance also was due to support from Kris Hemensley's Australian magazine *The Ear in a Wheatfield* and this searching around for support from other publishers echoed what had been achieved earlier, in 1973, when Douglas Oliver's *The Harmless Building* appeared as a joint venture of Grosseteste Review Books and Andrew Crozier's Ferry Press.

The murder of John Riley in Leeds took place in October 1978 and by November of that year Tim Longville had sent a sheet-long plea to all those interested in contributing some words for a memorial volume which would appear in the following year:

I want interested people to feel free to contribute in whatever way and at whatever length seems appropriate and possible to them. Let me say also that I don't want (because I don't think John would have wanted) a collection of unmitigated solemnities or pious admirations. He aimed always to use both his wits and his wit but was as aware as anyone that he sometimes *mis*-used them: so both laughter and honest reservations would seem to me to be entirely in his spirit and appropriate to our memories of him.

The thirty-five short reminiscences published in 1979 were presented in hardbound black with a black dust-wrapper. It was printed by Tony Ward of the Arc & Throstle Press, Todmorden, in an edition of three hundred copies and as Tim Longville explained in a small introductory note:

This book has not been edited. I let people know that the possibility of it existed: what is printed here is what was sent. I am deeply grateful both to those whose contributions are included and to the many others – too many to name – who have in a variety of ways helped its appearance.

Riley was forty-one years old when he died and he had been closely bound up with not only the setting up of the Grosseteste Press in 1966 but also with the second stage of setting up Grosseteste Review Books. Ric Caddell's contribution to the memorial volume voiced much of what was felt by the other contributors:

What in the world we see
is what's important. There
the days seemed shorter and our hearts
spun with the compass under

trees, magnificent pointers
out of galaxies. Continental drift,
an appointment we were late for,
an old friend missed.

The last years of the Grosseteste Review Press were taken up with Longville's monumental volume of Riley's *Collected Works* which appeared in 1980 and the last three volumes of *Grosseteste Review*. When volume fifteen appeared in 1983–84 it contained a valedictory comment:

For various reasons, too obvious to need explanation, this is the last issue of *Grosseteste Review*, at least in its present form.

Parting thanks: to surviving writers and readers for putting up with – and to surviving collaborators for helping to diminish – my manifest incapacity in most if not all of the many parts the production of the Review has pushed me to over the years.

I've enjoyed most of it most of the time. I hope you've enjoyed some of it some of the time.

In June 1983 Longville expressed some of his doubts about the future of the small press world to Michael Haslam:

No books sell now. I don't mean that they fail to sell out, I mean that to all intents and purposes they sell no copies at all. Certainly they do nothing like cover their costs. If anything, the 'audience' gets smaller with each attempt to tap it. I see little point in producing books more or less expensively in more or less extensive editions to lie mouldering in attics.

He concluded, 'Also I've been doing it for seventeen years. I'm tired. Let some other bugger have a go.'

The closing lines of Gordon Jackson's account stand as a reminder of the visionary quality of the setting up of the Grosseteste Press in Lincoln back in 1966:

[...] there was a hope and a struggle, in which participants saw themselves as amateurs and had no dreams of rewards, but who did what they did because it was a good thing to do... To us remain the pride, the memories, the delight in producing, and the still beauty of the products.

And that visionary quality is there in Jackson's own first book, *Dicta Lincolniensis*, a selection of the *Dicta Theologica* of Robert Grosseteste, produced on the original Grosseteste Press in 1972 in an edition of one thousand copies. He recalled it as a 'fine item' which was published 'under the Grosseteste imprint as I was still claiming *droits de seigneur*: But thereafter as two separate publishers were laying claim to the name I opted to work with a new imprint, and so the Asgill Press came into being.'

In 1997 Carcanet Press issued Jackson's *The Lincoln Psalter*, his 'Versions of the Psalms', with an Afterword written by Donald Davie who commended the founding of the Grosseteste Press as 'a rash and altruistic endeavour typical of the late 1960s at their best'.

A Charles Baudelaire Suite
translated from the French
DAISY FRIED

Autumn Song

Soon the plunge in dark and cold;
Goodbye too soon to summer's limpid light!
Already, I'm hearing firewood thump
Its hollow pavement shocks.

Winter feelings rush in: wrath,
Loathing, thrills of dread, sentence of hard labour,
And, like the sky in its polar hell,
My heart will freeze, a meaty block.

I shudder, listening to each log chopped.
A gallows being built has that muffled echo.
My mind's a teetering parapet
Annihilated by a battering ram below.

Rockabyed by this metronomic knock,
Seems someone hasty's nailing shut a coffin –
For whom? – it was just summer! now fall.
This odd noise rings out like loss.

*

I love the green light in your long eyes,
Comely one, but today I'm bitter,
And nothing, not our love, or bed, or hearth,
Is worth sunlight dappling the sea.

But darling! adore me. Be my daddy –
I'll be your naughty ingrate –
Or anyway, lover, brother, be the passing amity
Of autumn glory, setting sun.

Quick work. The greedy tomb awaits.
Ah, let me kneel, head resting on your knees,
To taste – grieving for burning summer –
These good late mellow yellow rays.

Auto Autumn

In the mirror, my own clear eyes say
'What, strange lover, is my merit?'
Shut up and charm me. Everything irks me
But ancient animal candour. My heart

Would hide its horrible secret,
Living lullaby whose hand strokes me to deep sleep,
Would conceal its fire-dark bedtime story.
I hate sex. It makes me sick.

Then let's love dispassionately. Cupid waits
in dark ambush, bending his fatal bow.
I know the machines of his ancient arsenal:

Crime, horror, madness! – oh pale flower,
Aren't you, like me, the sun in November?
So white, so cold, my Daisy?

The Sun

In an old faubourg where, hanging from hovels,
Jalousies hide languorous lust,
When cruel sun redoubles its drubbing
Of city and field, rooftop and wheat crop,
I'll joust out my loner fantasy,
Sniffing rhymes from every corner,
Tripping on words as over cobblestones,
To chance verses no one has ever dreamed.

Foster father, foe to anaemia, the sun
Raises worms and roses like verses in the fields,
Burns off care like mist to the sky,
Fills our minds and hives with honey.
It's he who lifts the spirits of men with crutches
Making them sweet and gay as girls,
And orders the harvest to ripen and thrive:
In the immortal heart, all's desperate to bloom.

When, like a poet, he goes down in the cities,
He dignifies the grubbiest, vilest things
And, relinquishing fanfare and servants, like a king
Inspects all the pesthouses and mansions.

Baudelaire's Cats

1.

Cat, come,
Sleek bewitcher,
Retract your claws
Into your paw pads.
Let me sink
In your beautiful eyes
Meld of metal
And agate.
When my fingers
Caress your nape
And supple back,
And my hand
Gets drunk
With the pleasure
Of touching
Your electric body,
I think of my man.
His stare, like yours, beast,
Deep, cold, cut
And split like a dart,
And head to foot
A subtle air,
A dangerous scent,
Swims around
His unknowable
Body.

2.

Lover or scholar,
Older, you admire
Cat sweetness
And cat power,
Pride of the home.
Gone torpid
And gun-shy
You sit by
The fire.
Familiar of science
And of pleasure,
He keeps to the dark side:
Silence. Horror.
Devil wants him
As doom-steed –
As if he could sell
Himself for that serfdom.
Behold, he muses
In poses of sphinxes
Lonely in the desert,
Submerged
In endless dream;
His loins are aglitter
With magic sparks
Like yours were;
And gold patches,
And fine sharp sand,
Star his mystic eyes.

3.

Through my brain,
Like it's his own backyard,
Strolls my charming cat,
His noise is profound, plush
And pearly, infiltrates
My darkest deeps,
Complicates like good poetry,
Settles me like a pill. He says
The manifold, needful things
Without a word, lullabies
My ecstasies of worry,
And thus as if with catgut bow,
Tunes my heart, his instrument.
From his motley fur
Comes a perfume so sweet
That one evening I thought
I was embalmed in it, having
Caressed him one time –
Just the once! He judges,
Presides, he inspires
All things in his empire.
Is he gremlin? Is he god?
Who shall say he is not
The happy genius of his household?
For when my eyes, obedient
To this cat I love, are pulled to him
As towards a magnet
I look inside myself.
Clear lanterns, pale eye-fire,
Living opals, fix me.

Owls

In black yew shelters,
Owls tuck themselves away,
Strange gods
With red meditating shifty eyes,

Otherwise roost unstirring
Till the melancholy hour
When darkness shovels
The sun offstage.

Thus, they teach the sage
She need fear in this world
Only tumult and action.

Passing, drunk on shadows,
My punishment for desiring change
Is desiring more change.

Reviews

On Seamus Heaney

On Seamus Heaney, Roy Foster
(Princeton University Press) £14.99
Reviewed by John McAuliffe

Part of Princeton's Writers on Writers series of 'brief, personal, and creative books in which leading contemporary writers take the measure of other important writers', Roy Foster's *On Seamus Heaney* (Princeton U.P.) is a short, curious addition to Heaney Studies and to Foster's own bibliography.

Foster is best known as a long-form writer on the late nineteenth and early twentieth century, and acknowledges that he is stretching himself to write about a direct contemporary. The opening page ponders his suitability for this project. 'I am acutely aware,' he writes, 'that I am far from possessing Heaney's gift to "glean the unsaid off the palpable,"' a statement which includes one of Foster's deftly sidestepping adjectives and a corrected, almost-correct quotation from Heaney's poem, 'The Harvest Bow'.

Pressing himself to make the case for his authority on the subject, Foster stakes his claim on autobiography and affect. Reading *North*, he felt that 'authentic sensation of the hairs standing up on *my head*' (an advance, maybe on the usual *back of the neck*); more recently, reading 'Album', 'his eyes filled with tears'.

The argument from affect might have prompted an interesting autobiographical essay, recounting Foster's own encounters with Heaney and his writing. The book *is* enlivened by those occasions, glancingly alluded to: Foster's pride in Heaney's performance as Oxford Professor of Poetry; his exchanges with the poet on W.B.Y. (the subject of Foster's brilliant two-part historical biography); meeting him in a London club at the unveiling of a portrait, in which the ageing Heaney can no longer see himself, an uncanny moment on which Foster might have elaborated.

But Foster, as a rule, excludes personal memories of the poet, and interviews none of their many mutual acquaintances. Instead he repeats the established narrative, from Bellaghy to London-Harvard-Oxford-Stockholm to Literature / Canon, drawing extensively on the work of predecessors, especially Dennis O'Driscoll's 'transactional biography' *Stepping Stones* (Foster's odd term for it), Heather Clark's group portrait, *The Ulster Renaissance*, and Richard Rankin Russell's student guide, *Seamus Heaney*, supplemented by grace notes from the archives deposited by Heaney in the National Library in Dublin. The writing generally stays close to the surface, linking poems to actual events, as if poems are cleverly slanted representations of what happened.

But there is nothing new here on the triggering contexts, or writerly exemplars or antagonists, nothing, say, on why his writing about sex and violence might chime with his friend John McGahern's censored, contemporary fiction; nothing on the globalising turn and cosmopolitan example of Derek Mahon, or on the widening influence of Eavan Boland.

It is surprising that this outstanding historian, whose work has persistently posed interesting, dialectical counterpoints and inspired speculations, has no such imaginative illumination to bring to Heaney. Here, as elsewhere in the critical undergrowth now straggling across Heaney's ouevre, *North* comes about as a result of reading P.V. Glob; *Death of a Naturalist* is about his childhood etc. And for such an experienced biographer, there is nothing on Heaney's own attempts at autobiography, on what drove him to start work on *Stepping*

Stones, or his intermittent and brilliant attempts to think about what is meant by autobiographical and confessional writing in essays on Hughes and Plath and Lowell.

Away from the terrain of life-writing, Foster is ill at ease in his discussion of the poems: a haiku, '1.1.87', is called 'haiku-like'. *Beowulf,* he relievedly declares, does not, 'mercifully, assert parallels between Beowulf's violent tussles in Denmark and the atrocities of twentieth-century Northern Ireland', but he says nothing about Heaney's astonishing introduction to that translation as an assault on the 'partitioned intellect' (a phrase of John Montague's for which Heaney reaches) and its pertinence to any 'late-twentieth-century news report, from Rwanda or Kosovo'. Reporting on the linguistic turn of the place-name poems, he happens upon 'A Northern Hoard', but somehow misses the estranging, scholarly note of its use of a word like 'spirochete' which may be said to characterize these poems as much as their Irish or Elizabethan elements. He extensively quotes sections of 'The Flight Path', first published in *PN Review* and dedicated to Donald Davie, but does not really explain why Heaney cut the quoted (stage-Irish) passages when he collected the book. He notices how the poem 'A Sofa in the Forties' picks up on images from Heaney's Nobel lecture, 'Crediting Poetry', but ignores that poem's references to news of Europe filtering in via a new radio, maintaining that 'Ghost train? Death gondola?'... 'seem to come from the fairground rather than, as some critics have suggested, the rail tracks to Auschwitz' (ignoring too that later poem about childhood, 'Polish Sleepers', which makes the same connection).

In its description of Heaney's style, a small band of adjectives, many to be found in overlapping thesaurus entries, is deployed and redeployed from chapter to chapter, within chapters, sometimes within paragraphs. Heaney is, repeatedly, 'strong', 'powerful', 'assertive', 'authentic', 'evocative' and 'prophetic', 'accomplished'. And as the book progresses, one verb stands in time and again to describe what the poems do: they 'interrogate', a verb which announces all kinds of blind spots and problems in Foster's conception of poetics, primarily because it suggests that the poems

exists in a posterior, critical relation *to* something, failing to recognise that Heaney's poems for fifty years crusaded on behalf of the poem's autonomy, its own thinginess, the idea that the lyric utterance arises out of an occasion, but somehow speaks beyond it, and belongs to any moment in which it is read, a poetics much scrutinised by other poets and, at length, in John Dennison's not uncritical *Seamus Heaney and the Adequacy of Poetry.*

The book refrains, though, from engaging with ideas, and operates by a series of close-ups, reporting on the poems and attempting to tally them with Heaney's movements. He usefully reminds us of Heaney's extra-literary activism, his participation in the Civil Rights marches, his service on the Arts Council during the 1970s, his public support for abortion rights in the 1980s, and his initial excitement about Field Day.

It is not quite right, either, to say that Foster's book is generally reliable on matters outside poetry. On the Irish-language context, he calls the self-admonishing poem 'Fill Arís' by Sean O Riordáin [sic] a 'controversial manifesto'. He is ambivalent about Field Day, as was Heaney, but surely unwise to say that Heaney was vital to 'attracting financial sponsorship, especially from American sympathizers'. *Sympathizers*!

When, in relation to this public whirl, he writes of Heaney's 'bedrock belief that the poet's vocation entailed an absolute need for privacy and independence', it is as if Foster has forgotten the poet's countervailing desire to live in the world, and how the latter acts in some way as a guarantor of the former. Too many poets would tell him they have all the privacy and independence they 'need'.

In one poem from his 'Lightening' sequence, Heaney admonished himself, 'Do not waver into language. Do not waver in it.' But the poet contradicts himself, and his poems do often waver, trying out one way, say, of looking at something which leads the poem and its reader somewhere else in poems which are, yes, eventually, assertive, accomplished, powerful and, in that uncanny way in which lyric poems work, both evocative and prophetic.

On Eavan Boland

The Historians, Eavan Boland
(Carcanet) £10.99
Reviewed by Kate Arthur

'My grandmother lived outside history' wrote Eavan Boland in her canon-breaking essay collection *Object Lessons*, 1996. 'And she died there.' It has been Boland's life work to draw attention to those silences and the parts they play in Irish history. As she returns to the figure of her grandmother in her final collection *The Historians*, there is a sense of weighing up the value of uttering the unsaid.

Seen as a whole, it can give the sense that it is a message brought from beyond the grave: not just with the wisdom of a life lived in commitment to the interrogation of poetry and of being a woman, but with the ghostly whisper of a spirit no longer subject to the forces they describe. There is a turn towards the earthly eternal – the rain, the light, the sea, the Wicklow hills and the light on them. There is a pervading sense of comfort from those things existing when we no longer do, or when we no longer utter them. There is a preference for silence, for just letting a day be itself. Indeed it brings silence, in the full range of its power: as omission, as repression, as forgetfulness, as resistance and as response to the ineffable, to the heart of the collection. 'The Just Use of Figures' opens with the lines 'Silence was a story, I thought, / on its own and all to itself.' Although it is a description of silence as an event, before a storm, this silence is the exemplar of Boland's poetic subject and mood.

The collection is in three parts and this poem is taken from the section entitled 'Three Ways in Which Poems Fail'. This admission of limitation, or lack, is explored in the first section 'The Historians' where the silence in the radiant, unforgettable poem 'The Fire Gilders' is of the mother's oral narration of her craft, held in Boland's memory, where it experiences decay. 'I learned,' she says, 'to separate memory from knowledge, / so one was volatile, one was not.' The grandmother evoked in 'Eviction' is not only silent in the record of the event, but in her contribution to the story of nationhood Boland has spent her career in (re)writing: 'A woman leaves a courtroom in tears. / A nation is rising to the light, / History notes the second not the first.' In 'Anonymous' the distant relative rumoured to have played her part in history by 'ferrying revolt' in secret messages she carried, her undocumented but active role in political events is contrasted with Boland's work 'This / is only poetry'.

In this way the collection is treading familiar Boland territory; concerned with nationhood, family and the role of the woman with in it, and the poetry within the woman, but in arresting ways it goes beyond it: to show the limitations of poetry, the impotence of her rage, and the danger of imagining a purity of form whether it be in the idea of a nation or of poetry. Yet the witness still matters: 'no one will remember I remember' ('Three Crafts').

Although the circumstances surrounding the creation of her last collection were so different, *The Historians* brings to mind Helen Dunmore's last collection, *Inside the Wave*, in its elegiac sense, its tender affection for the world that is being left behind, but a sense of acceptance of not being there to witness it. The clarity of her claim for the perspective of the powerless, as she says in 'Margin': 'telling the island, to myself, as I always have / so as to see it more clearly' gives her a claim to it: 'So I could stand, if only for one moment on its margin.'

On Sasha Dugdale

Deformations, Sasha Dugdale (Carcanet) £12.99
Reviewed by Declan Ryan

There are several layered worlds being constructed in Sasha Dugdale's latest collection, *Deformations*, its competing voices and stories all jostling for an attention they're usually denied. The abiding mood has to do with innocence, how vulnerable it is to exploitation, and the dark power it can afford to bad actors. *Deformations* is framed by two sequences, mythmaking (or un-making) in their impulse, the first ventriloquising and recasting the artist and illustrator Eric Gill, the second rendering Odysseus as 'Pitysad'. Both male leads are tricky, troublesome, – 'problematic', perhaps, in the current euphemistic parlance. Gill sexually abused his daughter, among other crimes, while the Pitysad we are presented lies, cheats and deceives on his interminable way home to Penelope, the moral centre of the poem, the voice of reason and humanity. This book is full of exceptional writing, on the small and grand scale, bristling with perfectly observed analogies, quiet, affecting music, subtly symbol-laden unpacking of difficult feeling. It opens with a breathtakingly unsettling poem, 'Girl and Hare'; on first-read, only an undercurrent of unease peeks through but, on re-reading, in the light of what is to follow, the red-lit and permeable line between child and creature: 'Hare had a narrow breast like hers, rosed with fur, and little childish shoulders / but forearms like a strong man's' takes on a far darker hue. There's something Nabokovian about Dugdale's ability to stare down unspeakable things in aesthetic terms throughout, to render the profoundly unpalatable in language which acts as a slow release alarm, none more so than in the Gill poems. The tawdriness of some of his reported speech, his talk of 'sex saliva' and 'slithering' stands in brilliant contrast with the matter-of-factness of a phoney chasteness, fiendishly well rendered, the quiet horror of the procession of girls making their Communion on 'a hay-fever day', 'everything ripe', is a striking achievement of control and composure.

The middle section of standalone poems has plenty of stand-out moments, too – not least 'Golden Age', as brilliant a portrait of thwarted ambition and self-deception as one could wish to read, the poet asking 'where was that prize, that prize / he was promised all those years ago / when he was driven by the fates / into the arms of time'. Fate and its driving impulses also shapes Pitysad's richly anachronistic tale, shuffling between a home for the insane, through scenes of highly modern PTSD, grooming a young girl in a foreign, sacked city with parcels of 'Shower gel / lipstick'. The urge is always to start over, if such were possible, rather than going back, or trying for repair after all the suffering and trauma – 'it is always easier to start in a new / place, thinks Pitysad'; 'Be quick and empty like a winecup, passed from mouth / to mouth.' Such is the engine of the great myths, and the great men of them, and it's this falsity and flattening which Dugdale wants above all to address. Her great achievement is in the nuance and compassion she brings to bear in the process, and in the final tumbling monologue which closes the sequence, itself perhaps a sly nod to another retelling of the Odyssey, Penelope has the final, deeply moving, word on the weight of living which stands behind the great eroding sweep of myth: 'if he could only bear it I would take that insignificant thing and I would love it with all my own insignificance. I'm insignificant but I've kept going...'. Tellingly, *Deformations* is dedicated 'for the insignificant' and by casting in such rich colour these apparently overlooked, marginalised, sinned-against voices Dugdale has done something which might, by a less sensitive writer, be called 'heroic'.

On Pablo Neruda

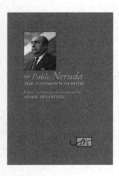

The Unknown Neruda, Pablo Neruda
translated by Adam Feinstein
Arc Publications, £10.99
Reviewed by Brian Morton

The title is immediately arresting, not just as Adam Feinstein says because Neruda was a Nobel prize-winner – plenty of laureates are honoured top-shelf busts but unread outside their domain – but because Neruda's global celebrity would seem to preclude anything being overlooked. And yet, there are many poems here that will only be known to specialists.

They come, even more intriguingly, from every phase of his career. Some of the most interesting, inevitably, are the early verses, some of them from notebooks entrusted, more than half a century after their composition and following the death of his half-sister Laura, to a presumed kinsman, subsequently auctioned and eventually published by Hernán Loyola in *Los cuadernos de Neftalí Reyes*, which put them beyond the reach of the average reader. They're revelatory to the extent that they immediately confirm that, for all his abundance of expression, Neruda took pains over every syllabic cadence and vowel sound. '*Adentro de mi vida voy echando mi ensueño / en lloviznas sutiles de amor y de veneno*' (*Lo Estéril*), rendered by Feinstein as 'My life is a daydream of / fine drizzle, love and poison', is a perfect early example and a good illustration of how confidently and un-fussily Feinstein has taken 'the tightrope walk between meaning and music'. Massively prolific he may have been, but there is not a sign of broad-brush writing anywhere. Even at the end, with something as white-hot as *Incitación al Nixoncidio y Alabanza de la Revolución Chilena* (An Incitement to 'Nixoncide' and Praise for the Chilean Revolution) he is incapable of writing without music.

Or, I've long believed, without the rhythms and the ritualised drama of Chile's national dance, the *cueca*, which regrettably only became such on the say-so of General Pinochet some years after Neruda's death. *Cueca* supposedly mimics the courtship movements of a cock and hen. Neruda had his chanticleer moments and even indulged a bit of hanky flapping when emotion, or more often, as in 'Severidad', pique overcame him. He often writes in a vibrant 6 / 8, a better way of thinking about his prosody than the usual metrics.

Early and late, Neruda has the perverse plenitude of Whitman and such an ability to contain multitudes that it is very difficult, as Feinstein concedes, to secure individual poems against any kind of biographical timeline. One certainly sees a turning outward – which is not quite the same as politicisation – after his diplomatic posting to Spain in 1934. He moved away from a poetry that was 'regional, painful and drenched in rain' (his own retrospective reckoning) towards the engagement (adhesiveness might be a better term and suitably Whitmanesque) of later years. It pleased him to allow visitors to continue believing that a portrait of Whitman on his wall was of a grandfather: a telling deception in more ways than one.

Feinstein's excellent introduction deals largely with textual matters, but is also an excellent primer on Neruda's life, influences and celebrity. It touches only passingly on the real origins of the Neruda name – Conan Doyle, a Czech writer and names of two violinists put together Pink Floyd-style have all been adduced – but more importantly includes the first poem to bear the new pseudonym in 1920, '*No seas como en árbol primifloro*', with the telling line '*La vida tuya / necesita de tierra removida / germinadora y buena.*' Here, the adjective really is untranslatable. Feinstein's 'restless' makes partial sense of Neruda's peripatetic life and mind, but '*removida*' has further associations of tillage that need to be understood as well.

To the standard complaint that the work is 'uneven', Feinstein simply repeats Nicanor Parra's devastating retort that the Andes are, too. One finds the soft-on-Stalin moments in the posthumous *Elegía* a little hard to understand, even at the forgiving distance of twenty years from the dictator's death, but more important in that late work is Neruda's insistence, addressed to/through Yevtushenko, that the poet's prerogative is to make mad jumps, without regard for consistency or social good. He is at the same theme in *Defectos Escogidos* which also came out in 1974. Feinstein's selection cleverly ends with '*El Gran Orinador*' in which some undefined almost Ubu-like figure pours endless stale on the people's heads and homes. The great urinator pisses on in silence. '*Qué quiere decir esto? // Soy un simple poeta, / no tengo empeño en descifrar enigmas, / ni en proponer paraguas especiales. // Hasta luego! Saludo y me retiro a un país donde no me hagan preguntas.*' (Poets aren't here to design umbrellas or solve puzzles. Hail and farwell! I'm off to where no one's going to bother me with questions.) That's the true voice of Neruda, passionately inexplicable and contrary. Whether for new readers or those who feel they had Neruda taped, Feinstein has created a highly thoughtful reappraisal, exactly what a good anthology should always do.

On Jean-Pierre Rosnay

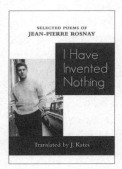

I Have Invented Nothing, Jean-Pierre Rosnay, translated by J. Kates
(Black Widow Press) US$19.95
Reviewed by Ross Cogan

As titles go, this has to be among the worst I've encountered. 'What,' I thought, 'nothing at all?' Surely poets owe us a little invention otherwise they risk becoming, in John Hollander's phrase, merely 'journalists of compassion'. I prepared to wade through what I assumed would be yet another volume of trite personal anecdotes and confessional verses that hardly needed confessing.

How wrong I was. Two things save this collection, indeed raise it into the realms of the memorable. Firstly, the title is clearly a lie. In fact, Rosnay was an unusually inventive, imaginative writer. Secondly, to the extent that he did draw upon his own experiences, he had the enormous advantage – rare among poets today – of having lived an interesting life.

Rosnay was born in 1926. When he was aged three his mother died; aged twelve he ran away from home to work on a farm; aged fifteen he started fighting with the French resistance. Shortly afterwards, having failed in his attempt to assassinate Klaus Barbie, he was incarcerated in an infamous military prison, from which, though wounded, he escaped. He was present – and wounded again – at the Battle of Saugues and the liberation of Le Puy. After the war, and a spell in the regular army, he headed for the Left Bank, where he founded a publishing house dedicated to bringing out the work of young poets, and later established the *Club des Poètes,* a bistro that doubled as a venue for poetry performances. At this time he was associated with such names as Boris Vian, Juliette Greco and Isidore Isou. Later he was to edit a major literary magazine, establish an international poetry festival and appear regularly on French radio and TV.

During his long life (Rosnay died in 2009) he published four substantial collections, two early in his career and two, following a thirty-four year hiatus, towards the end. In the early ones, though clearly influenced by the surrealism of Robert Desnos, Paul Eluard and Raymond Queneau, he often sounds like a French 'beat', as in 'Dead-End Road' from 1956's *Comme un Bateau Prend la Mer*:

Purple nights under bridges
With nothing to sleep on
Hard bread in black coffee
Among hookers and pimps
The German and the cop with
More than one trick up his sleeve

The reason for this, I suspect, is the influence on both of existentialism. Indeed, some of Rosnay's earlier

work seems almost a conscious attempt to sketch the shape of a poetics of authenticity and the avoidance of *mauvaise foi*. Take, for example, *Lorsque le matin est arrive, j'étais vivant*:

In a tree right across from me were two crows, I didn't even have to bother to make them up. I took my pencil and wrote a letter to Raymond Queneau, one of those letters you never send.

I was telling him, sir, I'm happy with myself, I'm not absolutely useless, I could have been able to accomplish much less than I have.

And even more I'm happy with you because you are curious and honest.

'Curious and honest' – these words perhaps best sum up Rosnay's early style, or at least the virtues that he wished his poetry to exhibit. This may make him sound naïve. It isn't intended to. It's more, I think, that he wanted to show Sartre's being-for-itself at work self-reflexively in the world – a self which can't watch a tree without watching itself watching a tree, as in *Quand un poète* from *Diagonales* (1960):

When a poet sees a chestnut tree
from a hotel window
He says I see a chestnut tree
from a hotel window
He picks out the chestnut tree
because in the ordinary course of
things
nobody notices

In the later collections, *Fragment et Relief* (1994) and 2002's *Danger Falaises Instables,* the poems are more expansive, both literally – they often spread over four or five pages – and metaphorically. They are much more likely to take the form of prose, particularly in the latter book. They also seem to draw more obviously from Rosnay's life story and a number deal with his experience in the resistance:

Of the forty of us who started out, seven are left. A good number, says Louis, but we never know when he's joking. Freddy's skull falls like a log split by an invisible axe. He was the only one of us who knew how to handle the four-wheel-drive

waiting down below in the farmyard where I had heard Freddy's voice for the first time; before the war, he was a waiter at La Coupole, that's all I know about him, now his body has fallen on the ground. (The Survivors)

Whether we see this as a prose poem or a short passage of conventional war memoir is surely beside the point – it's a powerful piece of writing. Where these later works take a more obviously 'poetic' form, they too are typically more relaxed and discursive, with longer lines and a more introspective tone, as in 'One Day':

One day I woke up saying to myself: Poetry isn't everything. It's one form of expression among others, an art that grows less and less popular.

One day I woke up saying to myself: poor bird, your whole life you've been hooked on that branch, you're a laughingstock!

I accused myself, insulted myself, called myself into question. One day, I went over to the enemy. I found myself ridiculous.

What had been everything to me my whole life long had become nothing.

You read me?

Even though you have a lot of other things to do?

Let's hope that we do. And Black Widow Press has provided an excellent starting point – a handsome parallel text containing a generous selection from all four collections. If Kates' translations perhaps lack a little *je ne sais quoi* (why, for example, choose the prosaic 'cry of an animal' for *cri de bête,* especially when, on the very next page, 'animals' is used to translate '*animaux*'?) they are still probably the best we will get, having been made in close cooperation with Rosnay and his wife, Marcelle. In any case, Rosnay's French is for the most part straightforward and direct – well within the reach of anyone with a dictionary who remembers some of their O Level or GCSE.

I've read somewhere Rosnay described as 'the last truly great poet to come out of France'. This is hyperbole. In fact he was a good minor poet, interesting both as a representative of his time and place and in his own right. And, as Eliot noted in *The Sacred Wood*, a good minor poet is 'something which is very rare'.

Three Translations

Menno Wigman, *The World by Evening*, translated by Judith Wilkinson (Shearsman Books) £12.95
Judita Vaičiūnaitė, *Vagabond Sun (Selected Poems),* translated by Rimas Uzgiris (Shearsman Books) £9.95
Mario Martín Gijón, *Sur(rendering),* translated by Terence Dooley (Shearsman Books) £10.95
Reviewed by Ian Seed

Although his name is relatively unfamiliar to the English-speaking world, Menno Wigman is one of Holland's most-acclaimed poets. He was born in 1966 in Beverwijk, and spent his childhood in the village of Santpoort. Nearby was a psychiatric institution, and, as Judith Wilkinson's compelling introduction informs us, the young Menno was fascinated by the patients who at times wandered about in the local woods. Throughout his life, Wigman expressed concern for people who live on the margins of society and who die forgotten and abandoned precisely by those who should be protecting them. Many of his poems feature such protagonists, such as the chillingly poignant 'Although We Know the Streets':

That's where the man had lain,
day in, day out –
they found him, darkened, eighty
newspapers late,
with on his chest the remnants of
a cat.

The irony here is that 'in that very same street you'll find a church / where cameras were installed the other week' – since all-seeing God cannot spot thieves.

Wigman's first collection to draw critical and popular attention was *In Summer All Cities Stink* (1997). In all, he published six full-length-collections, including a Selected Poems: *The Melancholy of Copy Centres*. He was active as an editor and translator from French and German, including the work of Baudelaire and Thomas Bernhard. As the poet wanders the streets of Amsterdam, his observations, bleak yet also full of yearning, can read like a those of a modern Baudelaire or Bernhard. The earlier work, especially, is haunted by a kind of bitter melancholy and resigned weariness as he examines himself, his relationships and the world around him. Fortunately, this is deliberately undermined by a sharp sense of irony and by a strict adherence to form. As the critic Marc Hurkmans pointed out, 'the poet never lapses into maudlin prattle about doom'. In a further act of self-subversion, Wigman makes sure that there are small technical deviations in his use of form, especially in the sonnets.

Wigman's aversion to modern life is expressed in the following manner in 'Last Taxi':

There is a ban on smoking now
and yet no one looks fresh.
We nurture a disgust that knows
no bounds.
A tender light shines in our
chatrooms. We have the right
to money, to sex, to bandages for
our brain stem.
You could say we're stripped of
Meaning – and what then.

And yet, on the last night of another year (and here he brings to mind Charles Bukowski's poem, 'palm leaves'), 'people are lighting fire-crackers, giving each other / famous kisses. I look. I see. Will live.' And it's important to note that Wigman does not in any sense see himself as separate from, or superior to, modern life. As he says in his poem 'Burger King':

If there was a time when I was
above it all,
my mouth full of Proust and
Yeats, you won't
hear me now.

Judith Wilkinson's translations are rendered with great craft and painstaking attention to detail. They read naturally yet also preserve much of the musicality of the originals (the Dutch versions are published alongside the English), as well as their structure and (half) rhyme-schemes. Wigman gave Wilkinson a free hand, but also gave feedback on her draft translations of his work. On 1 February 2018, just a week after Shearsman accepted the translations, Wigman died of heart failure at the age of fifty-one.

Judita Vaičiūnaitė (1937–2001) was a major Lithuanian poet of the second half of the twentieth century, one of a generation of poets who in different ways used their creative work in subtle ways to express resistance to Soviet rule and Communist ideology, for example an emphasis on the subjective world of the poet. Her family moved to Vilnius after the Second World War. The printed Lithuanian word had in fact been banned by czarist Russia, and so writing in Lithuanian was a way to preserve a nation and its culture. As Rimas Uzgiris outlines in his comprehensive introduction, one of the cultural differences between Lithuania and the West, which is important to understanding Vaičiūnaitė's poetry, is the relative persistence of neo-romantic strains in Lithuanian literature right up until the twenty-first century. As well as a focus on subjective experience, her early poems sometimes contrast the ideal of nature and traditional country life with modern alienation, and hark back to Lithuania's past. However, Vaičiūnaitė soon 'came to adapt her poetics to urban existence, breaking apart her lines in stanzas, building run-on sentences on top of each other, connecting (or disconnecting) phrases with dashes, using ellipses to create pauses and gaps', making her one of the most innovative poets of her generation. Her work is sensory and meditative at the same time, the images precise and yet at times so compact that they almost but not quite blur into one another, producing an eerie and haunting lyricism in their portraits of city life, or of trips away from the city, for example in the sequence, 'Room on the Dunes':

But the film goes on. The birds
perch on my shoulders.
        Delayed in their dark cries, I
                             feel
bright trains stopping behind our
                             backs
    in the asphalt town.
And foreign, shabby furniture
                          shivers
    in the room on the dunes –
                          amazed
    that I'm smiling, hiding my eyes
        in the hot, dry palms of
                    your hands.

Many of the poems explore female
desire, either through the poet's own
experience, or through adopting the
voices of historical or mythical charac-
ters, such as the women in the life of
Odysseus, their voices by turn full of
desire, or loss or gentle mockery.
While Odysseus's abandoned lovers
yearn for him, the 'boring and eccen-
tric Penelope' offers to 'wipe away the
blood from your hands / using my very
own hair, my lips' ('Four Portraits').
Throughout this collection, Rimas
Uzgiris has sought to maintain the
musicality of the original versions, not
an easy endeavour given the complex-
ities of the Lithuanian language.

Mario Martín Gijón's *Su (rendering)*
is a traditional story of love lost and
found, but he tells the story through
a process of linguistic invention and
playfulness, so that, in the words of
translator Terence Dooley, the 'lan-
guage of love' becomes as 'fraught
with contradiction as love itself'.
Gijón deliberately creates ambiguity
and multiple possible meanings –
harking back to the Cubists' ambition
to paint the same object from differ-
ent perspectives within the same pic-
ture – by the insertion of brackets
around letters, slashes allowing a
choice between letters, dashes sever-
ing or connecting syllables, and by
suffixes or prefixes belonging equally
to the words surrounding them:

s(u/e)rv(ey)ing you gave
me hope and strength to
cont(ai)n(yo)ue
giving my word ploughed
ground
following the furrows
of your abs(c)ent
body
(from 'the promise of (as) saying
you')

Here the narrator is not only navigat-
ing loss but also, in a phenomenolog-
ical approach, examining the way his
own consciousness is fractured into
different possible responses to a sit-
uation where his sense of being a self
has been shattered.

There are also moments of pure lyr-
ical intensity amongst all the ambi-
guity, which one feels grateful for as
one would when coming across a
clearing in a dense dark forest:

it started to rain on my window
in the pathways of my dream
and
the ghost of you came close [...]
a promise of imminence
sudden and fresh as rain on sleep
(*from* 'pre-sentiment, night')

Terence Dooley's translation strays
a little too far at times from the Span-
ish original, but at least succeeds in
conveying the complex lyricism of the
original.

It is good in these times of nation-
alist politics to see the way poetry
translation continues to thrive.

On Robert Selby and Michael Vince

The Coming-Down Time, Robert Selby
(Shoestring Press) £10.00
Long Distance, Michael Vince
(Mica Press) £8.99
Reviewed by Kevin Gardner

In an age of social distancing, poetry
seems more vital than ever for forging
connections across rifts in time and
space. Two new collections – one by
a seasoned poet, pensive and subtle;
the other a dazzling debut from the
editor of *Wild Court* – amply bridge
past and present, the remote and the
immediate. While their voices are
uniquely their own, Robert Selby and

Michael Vince share common fea-
tures in their collections, including an
interest in obscurer corners of erst-
while England – rural Suffolk in the
early twentieth century; a Victorian
London suburb – yet remoteness is
made present through their gripping,
even startling scenes, the accessibili-
ty of their language, control of formal
elements, and the reworking of pas-
toral tradition.

In his opening poem, Robert Selby
establishes the spirit that invigorates
The Coming-Down Time. His 'Chapel'
ancestors, 'owning no graveyard, / are
permitted to join the heaped-up past
/ among St Bartholomew's windswept
grass / during a terse, wind-scattered
prayer'. Permeated by a sense of land-
scape, history, family, and divine
intention, Selby's collection is a three-
part lyrical meditation on the forces
that define individual and national
identity. 'East of Ipswich' memorialises
the poet's ancestors, especially his
grandparents, while 'Shadows on the
Barley' contains persona poems, ele-
gies, and poems of personal reflection
and relationships; the final section,
'Chevening' – ostensibly a country-
house sequence – embodies the inter-
twining of personal experience and
social history. 'All of it evocable at a
whiff of buddleia. / It wreathed the
dead, straightened the steeple, /
placed the fielders, re-glazed the red
phone box.' At the core of *The Coming-
Down Time* is a double helix of con-
stancy and change. A bygone world
endures, and what prevails is a san-
guine hope in the present.

The poet's grandfather – the last of
'a long line of men who worked /
now-extinct equine trades: wheel-
wright, ostler, / coachman, horseman'
– provides the unifying force in the
first section as the grand narrative of
twentieth-century England is woven
with personal stories. For an agri-
cultural labourer, a lunch of 'rabbit, /
suet pudding' carries 'no risk of calo-
ries dawdling to fat'; the real risk to
such a labourer is sociological as trac-
tor displaces plough. Startled by a
belching engine on a twilit farm, he
is bemused by the sudden appearance
of 'an unblinkered beast / braying
smoke in the top field', and contem-
plates the revolutionary significance
of 'light / from its side-lamps shining
off makers' plates / cast from melted-
down horse brasses'. History again

resonates privately when a chivalrous act begets a romance. Selby's grandparents, not yet married, are waiting for a bus when a German V-bomb drops: 'He pulled her down, throwing himself on top of her' and not long thereafter she 'became a doting wife and mother, and grandmother'. When the story is repeated at his grandmother's funeral, Selby permits a brief, intimate glimpse of his grandfather's grief for the woman 'whom he couldn't shield with his body / the final time'.

Such poignant moments are matched by lines that mesmerise with rhythmic beauty ('Spring's breeze silvered the birches / burgeoning greenly'; 'a tide over shingle in your voice') and by stanzas of formal intricacy. Potent images persist, catching in one's throat after the reading ends – 'knitted limbs of knotted fabric' caught on a wintry brier; a WWI soldier's bicycle left beside a village sycamore, the tree grown round it, now 'clutching to its bark the spokes and saddle'; a cherry tree, root-loosened by winds and leaning precariously, sending up 'rod-straight new boughs / ... skyward in corrective pursuit / to self-sustain its standing'. Woven throughout are ruminations on mutability, in which Selby wonders – here, addressing the composer George Butterworth, killed at the Somme – 'if the feelings the late violin sends through me / are now commonly shared, if they ever were, / and what exactly they are – like England, // cow parsley in the wheat, and the Glorious Dead, / if that is England.' Yet melancholy is counter-balanced with an enduring hope, as in this vision of WWI soldiers returning home from battle, and bringing with them a renewal of life: 'They move into the field-sweet air; the women turn / from sheaving, rush disbelieving to their dearest ones // Their names our father bore, then us; now our sons.'

The disruption of memory is likewise a robust motif in Michael Vince's *Long Distance*. His poems tend to move in one of two directions: either into the past (to nineteenth-century Camberwell and further back, to a Jacobean country house, the medieval palace of Eltham, and the Saxon *bocland*) or into the self (with meditative explorations of himself, others, and his relationships). Like the Saxon

charter in 'Bookland', Vince's poems are 'illuminated, / faintly on time's over-sanded palimpsest'; indeed, he excels at recouping lost memory. 'The Lava Rink', for instance, revivifies a long-gone roller-skating arena and the lively colour of Victorian social pleasures; now all that remains is an empty field above a rail tunnel, 'a buried thought fading // one more cold stain warming into memory'. A ruined suburban mansion springs back fully to life in 'Last Gate Post', 'the surviving invisible / empty gate through which a past place shows / its outline, its faded structure the mockery / of a living creature uncovered by explorers / on a hostile world'. 'Faded' and 'fading' recur through the collection, and the evanescent past is salvaged wherever Vince finds it. At certain moments, however, the past's endurance proves tiresome to the poet, who is perturbed 'that things don't vanish, / that stubborn traces cover me over / with patches of yellow patterning'.

This troubling idea that the past never disappears, only fades, recurs in Vince's elegant poems of personal reflection. In 'Long Distance', lovers' voices are 'stilled but unsilenced'; more disconcerting is the discrepancy between lovers' memories in 'House on the Shore': 'your memory has dropped through / a crack in time just leaving one loose thread. / I hold on to one end of it and pull.' A particularly affecting variation of this incongruity is 'Body Swerve'; here the poet confesses that although 'my body held constant / urgent course with yours', he wonders if perhaps the gesture was dishonest: 'did my eyes signal / one way, while the rest of me / went the other?' Arriving at an ambiguous conclusion relevant to any consideration of the transient past, he wonders 'if part of the mind deceives itself, / swerving from truth to hope and back'. This concept gains a numinous intensity in 'The Ordinary', depicting an encounter with a Greek fisherman, priestly in appearance, who 'raised a hand, palm open, / in a muted blessing, or so it seemed'. It's impossible not to be stirred by Vince's assessment of 'ease on the edge of ordinariness / where it touches the matters of the soul, the mystery / of our coming and going'. This mystery is at the heart of both of these entrancing collections.

On Leeanne Quinn and Rachael Allen

Some Lives, Leeanne Quinn (Dedalus Pres) €12.50
Kingdomland, Rachael Allen (Faber) £ 10.99
Reviewed by Aoife Lyall

Leeanne Quinn's intimate and astute second collection, *Some Lives*, is suffused with the paired sensations of passing through and being passed through: the sense of the body as both a solid and a stateless thing; as fundamental to our being as it is extrinsic to our worth.

Many of the poems within confront loss, and the struggle to articulate the emptiness of absence. Quinn speaks to small, hard truths beyond our grasp: 'I have found the records, / checked its phase on your date of birth / and mine, now that you are no age' ('January'). She recognises the paradoxes through which we attempt to reconcile the unfathomable – 'I think of the you that is / and is not' ('Other Worlds'); and with that, the lonely need to turn an echo into a conversation; 'O how we both know precisely // more than the other now — you, / how to go, me, how to go without' ('Smoke'). And, ultimately, how it all comes down to guilt: the guilt of still being able, even willing, to live without them: 'As I write / I am almost ashamed to let you know / I am here and still alive' ('Any Weather').

Loss can often leave us as separated from the living as it does from the dead: 'I never knew the world as something / to be in, until it pushed me out' ('Shells'). In her position as outsider, Quinn takes up the mantle of observer, and inquisitor. In 'The Distant Past' she posits the question 'but why should I expect to be happy?' – and wonders how we have yet to determine a reason for our existence in 'Cave of the Firbolg', 'Nobody thinks, Why do we do this?' She also speaks to more personal fears, such as those that come with the lessening of grief – 'Is used to the same as forgetting?' ('January') and an inability to recapture the everyday courage to face life's incumbent uncertainties: 'Winter, / was I always this afraid?' ('Smoke').

So much of any life is repetition and Quinn's dexterous and insightful use of rhythm and rich rhyme creates a cajoling and disconcerting undercurrent in *Some Lives*. Several of the poems move forward as they pull the reader back: sometimes this is done to encourage a new perspective, as in 'Not at All Like the Sea' – 'And what kind of silence is the silence / of seeing the sea behind glass as white / waves crash without sound, without'; likewise, in 'Some Lives', 'Some cities bury their dead upwards / in high-rise vaults. If a cemetery is an inverted city / then this is an inversion of that.' Other times, it is used to eschew easy interpretation, such as in 'Elegy':

Nobody died nobody mourned
we love a kill we love a kill
we love a kill and we love nothing
    more
than to mourn but nobody died

The collection's eponymous poem makes up a significant portion of the book. Embodying fragments of other poems, its antepenultimate position gives 'Some Lives' a sense of solidarity, grounding and reassuring both reader and poet as they navigate the lives, and lives lost, across its twenty pages. Worthy of further and sustained exploration, *Some Lives* evokes the otherness of loss with an ethereal quality, one that captures the essence of what it means to live without those whose existence is so essential to our own.

*

Kingdomland is an inferno, a surreal forge within which language, structure and meaning exist at a perpetual melting point: one that takes the familiar, the comfortable, and reshapes it into the surreal, as in the title poem:

Small white socks bob into the
dark like teeth in the mouth
of a laughing man, who walks
backwards into night,
throwing drinks into the air
like a superstitious wife throws salt.

This is a collection that burns as it builds. The female body is neither a delicate nor curious thing, but an object. It is a thing to be penetrated: 'I played a ham-fisted stick-in-the-mud / Let him stick it where the sun don't shine' ('No last kiss'); aggravated 'For a laugh I told him he was adopted, / brother Daniel, and he beat me to a pulp' ('Simple Men'); and incinerated 'I was one burnt daughter / in a genealogy' ('Apostles Burning'). It is a carnal thing, devoid or detached from the idylls of the body as a temple, a tabernacle of the self. Here it is nothing more than something to be reduced, reused and recycled, the contents deemed irrelevant, immaterial, or already used up:

this is just what happened to me
I suppose it happens to many
    others
if you wear pink dungarees
at an amiable age
[...]
in the end he would barely touch me
were I to stay long enough to
scrape dark butter
onto toast.
('And the face in the mirror, no
longer familiar')

Blood flows through *Kingdomland*. Here, the woman's body, the girl's body, the menstruating body is portrayed as abhorrent, an affront to civilised society:

where only girls lived, carbuncled
in dust,
caught mid-play and mid-menses,
long arms
chastising or rubbing filth on
themselves, arched
over desks and on the swings,

illicitly being. ('Volcano')

Allen calls out the taboos surrounding periods, with their pervasive beliefs and the punishments meted out to the girls in retribution for the impurity the process supposedly imparts. The coercive myth of the precious pregnancy is also forcefully decried, one that leaves so many women who experience pregnancy loss writhing in contrition at their secret relief:

Intestinal scorching, a stomach of
shavings.
Being haunted by a baby is worse
than you'd think. I don't want her,
an ingrown ghost, intermittent
horror,
('Seer')

Kingdomland is a visceral dreamscape, one in which verse fragments and sequences are juxtaposed in non-linear narratives from which we may form any number of unrealities. Allen adheres to no strict form or formula. These poems are the ashes of expectations and beliefs; built over hundreds of generations, *Kingdomland*'s battle cry is clear:

counting all the dead women
putting them in a document

burn all documents
rescue the women
('Landscape for a Dead Woman')

And so it is fitting that these poems self-immolate and avoid the pitfalls and pigeonholes of traditional models. Expect, then, to read this collection on its own terms; Allen does not include notes to light the reader's way, not when she herself is still waiting for someone to 'tell me on the phone just once something that will feel like / a small match striking at the base of my neck' ('What a summer we had'). *Kingdomland* is for those who want revolution, not revelation.

Contributors

Tony Roberts's fifth collection, *The Noir American & Other Poems*, was published in 2018. His second book of essays on poets, poetry and critics, *The Taste of My Mornings*, appeared in 2019. Both are from Shoestring Press. **Olivia Byard**'s first collection was a Forward prize nominee. Her third book of poems, *The Wilding Eye*, published in 2015, became a *New Statesman*'s chosen read. Following that, her work became represented on the US hypertext site. **Michael Heller** has published over twenty-five volumes of poetry, essays, memoir and fiction. Recent books include *Constellations of Waking*, an opera libretto on Walter Benjamin, and *Telescope: Selected Poems*. **Kevin Gardner** is Professor and Chair of English at Baylor University. With John Greening, he has edited *Hollow Palaces*, an anthology of modern country house poems, forthcoming from Liverpool UP. **Sarah Wedderburn** works as a writer for arts and architectural projects and lives near Canterbury. She holds a degree from Oxford University and a Poetry School MA from Newcastle University. **Ian Seed**'s latest collections are *The Underground Cabaret* (Shearsman, 2020) and *Operations of Water* (KF&S, 2020). He is currently working on a translation of Max Jacob's *The Dice Cup*, due out from Wakefield (USA) in 2023. **Declan Ryan**'s latest pamphlet, *Fighters, Losers* (New Walk), was published in 2019. **Colm Tóibín** is the author of nine novels, including *Brooklyn* and *The Master*, and two collections of stories. He is Chancellor of the University of Liverpool. **Alexey Shelvakh**, born 1948, published many stories in the pioneer publications of Leningrad. Later he worked as a lathe operator, publishing poetry and prose in major *samizdat* magazines. Since the 1990s, he has been an editor and translator (mainly of fantasy) in the St. Petersburg publishing houses Azbuka and Amphora. **Vahni Capildeo** is Writer in Residence at the University of York. Recent work includes *Like a Tree, Walking* (Carcanet, forthcoming), *The Dusty Angel* (Oystercatcher, forthcoming), and *Light Site* (Periplum, 2020). **Togara Muzanenhamo** was born in Zambia and brought up in Zimbabwe. He studied Business Administration in France and the Netherlands. He lives with his partner and two children. **Miles Burrows** trained at Oxford. He was a doctor in Chimbu Highlands New Guinea, and among Hmong tribe refugees on the Thai/Laos border, and in Taiwan. He worked as deck-hand in Iceland at midwinter. **Madeleine Pulman-Jones** studies Russian and Spanish at the University of Cambridge. Her poems have appeared in *The Adroit Journal* and *The Mays Anthology*, among other publications. **John Robert Lee** is a Saint Lucian writer. His *Collected Poems 1975–2015* (2017) and *Pierrot* (2020) are published by Peepal Tree Press. **Alex Wylie**'s published work includes *Secular Games* (Eyewear, 2018), his debut poetry collection, and *Geoffrey Hill's Later Work: Radiance of Apprehension* (Manchester University Press, 2019). **David Herman** is a regular contributor to *PN Review*. He is a freelance writer based in London who writes mainly on Jewish European and American writing and criticism. **Aoife Lyall**'s debut collection *Mother, Nature* will be published by Bloodaxe Books in 2021. The writing of her second collection is being supported by the National Lottery through Creative Scotland. **Camille Ralphs**'s pamphlets are *Malkin* (The Emma Press, 2015) and *Uplifts & Chains* (If a Leaf Falls Press, 2020). She is the Poetry Editor at the *TLS*. **Lisa Kelly**'s first collection *A Map Towards Fluency* is published by Carcanet. Her pamphlet *From the IKEA Back Catalogue* will be published by New Walk Editions in 2021. **Tara Bergin** is from Dublin and has published two collections with Carcanet, *This is Yarrow* (2013) and *The Tragic Death of Eleanor Marx* (2017). She now lives in the North of England and is working on her third book. The title of **John Lucas**'s new novel, *The Life in Us*, due in April, is taken from Anne Stevenson's poem 'An Even Shorter History of Nearly Everything'.

Colophon

Editors
Michael Schmidt
John McAuliffe

Editorial Manager
Andrew Latimer

Editorial Assistant
Charlotte Rowland

Contributing Editors
Vahni Capildeo
Sasha Dugdale
Will Harris

Design
Cover and Layout
by Emily Benton Book Design

Editorial address
The Editors at the address on the right. Manuscripts cannot be returned unless accompanied by a stamped addressed envelope or international reply coupon.

Trade distributors
NBN International

Represented by
Compass IPS Ltd

Copyright
© 2021 Poetry Nation Review
All rights reserved
ISBN 978-1-78410-836-6
ISSN 0144-7076

Subscriptions—6 issues
INDIVIDUAL–print and digital: £39.50; abroad £49
INSTITUTIONS–print only: £76; abroad £90
INSTITUTIONS–digital only: from Exact Editions (https://shop.exacteditions.com/gb/pn-review)
to: PN Review, Alliance House, 30 Cross Street, Manchester, M2 7AQ, UK.

Supported by